RISK ASSESSMENT
IN PEOPLE WITH
LEARNING
DISABILITIES

Author's Note

All the cases described in this book, while based on clinical experiences of the author, are fictitious, and any apparent likeness to any real person, whether living or dead, is purely coincidental.

carol sellars

RISK ASSESSMENT IN PEOPLE WITH LEARNING DISABILITIES

BPS Blackwell

© by Carol Sellars 2002
A BPS Blackwell book

Editorial Offices:
108 Cowley Road, Oxford OX4 1JF, UK
Tel: +44 (0)1865 791100
350 Main Street, Malden, MA 02148–5018, USA
Tel: +1 781 388 8250

First published 2002 by The British Psychological Society and Blackwell Publishers Ltd, a Blackwell Publishing company

Library of Congress Cataloging-in-Publication Data

Sellars, Carol Wedel.
  Risk assessment in people with learning disabilities / Carol Sellars.
    p. cm.
Includes bibliographical references and index.
  ISBN 0–631–23547–7 (pbk. : alk. paper)
  1. Learning disabilities. 2. Risk assessment I. Title.
  RC394.L37 S445 2002
  616.85′889—dc21

                                                2002000710

A catalogue record for this title is available from the British Library.

Set in 10/12pt Photina
by SetSystems Ltd, Saffron Walden, Essex
Printed and bound in Great Britain
by MPG Books, Bodmin, Cornwall

For further information on
Blackwell Publishers, visit our website:
www.blackwellpublishers.co.uk

CONTENTS

chapter one

ASSESSMENT OF RISK IN PEOPLE WITH LEARNING DISABILITIES: WHY IS IT NEEDED?

A Normal Life: What Is It?

In recent years the majority of people with learning disabilities (who were not already living with their families), have moved out of the old long-stay hospitals into the community. Most of these have moved into smaller homes, sometimes purpose-built, sometimes conversions of ordinary housing in local communities. Some have moved into flats or other relatively independent living situations where they receive the support they need to live alone, or with a friend or partner. People with learning disabilities are beginning to reclaim the lives they lost in the institutions, having choices, jobs, sex lives and even becoming parents – unthinkable until even quite recently. Slowly, perhaps far too slowly, the rest of the community is beginning to realize that the majority of people with learning disabilities are not so different from everyone else, and need the same things in their lives that all of us do: work, leisure, partners, and a sense of being part of a social group. They want to feel useful and valued, as we all do.

Sadly, this new freedom is not yet available to everyone with learning disabilities. Because of their very real difficulties in coping with everyday life, some people with learning disabilities still have to rely heavily on others to help them live what we would call a normal life. For some this reliance is almost complete. This means that their choices often remain limited because they not only need help with everyday activities but also to make the choices and decisions that we all make as part of a normal life. Nevertheless, we should be trying to ensure that all people with learning disabilities are able to have as much of a normal life as possible. But what is a 'normal' life?

Most of us live in a place we choose, with people with whom we choose to share our lives. We have a job, and we spend our leisure as we please. Of course very few of us have the amount of choice in these matters that we would ideally like to have. Jobs may be hard to come by. The standard of housing may be lower, and money available less, than we want, and relationships do not always work out as we would like. However, few of us would let someone else choose our housemates, or our job, even if these are less than ideal.

At a simpler level, we can usually have some choice over what we eat, or what we wear. We can eat what we want, usually when we want. We choose our clothes and when to get dressed, even if others do not always approve of what we wear. We may have to get up at a time that is determined by the needs of a job, at least in the week, but at weekends we can usually get up when we like, and most of us can go to bed when we like. In our free time we can usually go out when we want, and with whom we want. If we want to go out and get drunk, we can do so, cash permitting. If we stay at home, we usually have some say in what we watch on TV, or indeed whether we watch it at all. If we feel like spending the evening in bed, or reading quietly alone, then most of us can do that, at least sometimes. We go shopping, and choose the things we want, again cash permitting! So an ordinary life, while it has some restrictions, generally includes a fair amount of choice.

Services for people with learning disabilities have increasingly accepted that their clients have a right to make choices and decisions, and structure their organization and the care it provides accordingly. Unfortunately, much of this choice depends on the availability of social service funding, and the type and quality of care staff available, so that many people with learning disabilities still have considerably less choice than they should have.

In spite of these difficulties, there is an increasing awareness that people with learning disabilities can make choices, and moreover they want to do so. However, what we often fail to consider is the amount of risk that these choices carry. Most of us have grown up accustomed to risk-taking. Going to bed very late carries the risk that we are too tired to get up for work the next day. If we do that too often, we may lose our jobs. Going out drinking carries the risk that we may make ourselves ill by over-indulgence, or crash the car on the way home because our drunkenness makes it impossible to control it properly. Even crossing the road carries a significant risk.

Most of the time, we do not think about these risks. We calculate risk on our own behalf all the time, but because we do it so frequently it is rarely consciously considered. Generally, we tend to underestimate the level of risk, especially when activities are familiar. It is only when a risk is brought to our attention that we give it serious conscious thought. Research indicates that education about a particular risk often increases people's estimation of the likelihood of an undesirable consequence occurring, at least in the short term. In recent years, the risk of salmonella poisoning from eggs, the risk of contracting HIV from unprotected sex, and the risk of eating beef which may give us CJD have all been drawn to our attention. Many of us are now aware of these particular risks, and because the media have emphasized them, we may therefore give these risks greater weight than they deserve. It has been said, for example, that the risk of developing CJD is several times less than the risk of being struck by lightning, but many people stopped eating beef because of their fear of taking this risk.

Life is full of risks. We all take risks all the time, and the more familiar they are the less we tend to recognize the real level of risk involved. We actually take the greatest risk in our lives every time that we step into a car, but few of us really consider that risk seriously. This is the other side of the coin; we are inclined to believe that 'it won't happen to me', even when the objective statistics suggest otherwise.

Moving into Community Settings: Benefits and Risks

As discussed above, the benefits of moving into community settings are many. For those who grew up in the old 'mental handicap' hospitals, community living suddenly offers a whole new range of choices and benefits: new activities, new friends, the chance to work, and most importantly the opportunity to make choices about these things. Even choice about the more mundane things such as what to wear, what time to go to bed, and what to eat can seem exciting, if the opportunity to make these choices is a new experience.

However, along with this freedom to make choices come the risks that we all share. If people choose to eat chocolate all the time, they will get fat, and become unhealthy because of the lack of a good diet. This may lead to serious illness in time. How far should choice go? When do we have a duty of care to intervene because of the risks involved? Would we feel this responsibility to intervene if the person concerned did not have a learning disability?

For those who have the responsibility of caring for people with learning disabilities, there is a difficult tightrope to walk between allowing choice and associated risk-taking, and yet not forgetting the duty of care that such a role imposes. In law, those who take on a duty of care have a responsibility to protect their clients from harm, and they run the risk of being accused of negligence if they do not do so. Most carers tend to err on the side of caution because of this.

Usually we assess our own personal risks in terms of gains. We tend to balance the short-term gains against the long-term gains, and then make a decision about whether the risk is worth it. Most of us do this automatically, and without much effort. We may not always make the 'best' decisions in terms of our long-term good, because for most of us short-term gains are more powerful motivators than long-term ones: the pleasures of smoking may outweigh the long-term health risks of doing so. We may know that there are risks, but deny them by being selective about the information we read, or dismissing the research that identifies these risks as faulty. We weigh our own experiences more heavily against such 'official' risks: 'My grandfather smoked all his life and he lived to be 95.' Or we may accept the risk as real but simply say to ourselves that the short-term pleasures are worth it. After all, it is not certain that we will get lung cancer if we smoke. It might happen, but it might not. Generally we like to believe it will not.

Where the long-term risk is greater or the consequences are more undesirable, then we may forgo the short-term gain. Unprotected sex may not only lead to HIV infection (low risk) but also to pregnancy (high risk). Thus most of us take some kind of contraceptive measures, but may not practice 'safe sex' in the recommended manner, even while recognizing that sex with a new partner might result in HIV infection. Some people, including those of normal ability, will happily take both risks, blithely assuming that they are somehow immune to the risks involved.

People with learning disabilities are subject to the same risks as all of us, but unfortunately they may also be subject to additional risks. They may be bullied or abused by those who have control over them, or by those who realize that they are vulnerable, and because of their disabilities they often find it very much more difficult to assess risk in the way that most of us do. While most of us do not assess risk very efficiently, we generally make some attempt to do so. It is a complex task, and most of the time we do it adequately but not very thoroughly. People with learning disabilities also find this difficult but may also fail to recognize any risk at all. They therefore have particular problems in coping with risky situations and decisions, either because they have not had the same learning opportunities as the rest of us, or because the task of assessing risk in relation to their own activities is too difficult for them.

Choices and Responsibilities: Legal, Moral and Social

Every choice we make carries implications. Sometimes these implications involve a high risk, sometimes a negligible one. We learn these implications in a variety of ways. Often this is from our own experience, sometimes it is from others, and sometimes it is from the media or from books. Many people with learning disabilities have been denied the opportunity to learn from their own experiences. Either the experiences themselves have been unavailable or denied them, or they have been so overprotected that the chance to learn by experience has not been there. This makes it impossible for the person to make a real choice, because they do not know what the alternatives are, or the risks that each alternative carries.

It is important that, when making choices about their lives, people with learning disabilities have the opportunity to learn about the implications of their decisions. Legally, some choices carry a penalty. For example, if a person chooses to seek sexual satisfaction from children, they will come into conflict with the law. Some people with learning disabilities lack information and understanding about how the law works, and may not appreciate that some behaviours can result in their being locked up. In making decisions about life choices such as marriage, people with learning disabilities need to understand, like the rest of us, that getting married carries legal as well as social responsibilities. It is important that someone with learning disabilities who is about to make a decision which carries a legal implication is made aware of this, and understands exactly what it can mean for them.

A further legal complication is the responsibility that the law places on carers who have accepted a duty of care by accepting their job. This implies certain standards of care which can be seen as essential by a court, in cases where negligence is alleged. It is important that when choices are being made, the people involved, both the client and others involved in his or her care, have actively considered the likely gains and losses. There is a tendency to assume 'risk' always implies something negative. However, sometimes taking a risk can have a positive result; gambling on the Lottery may mean you lose your money, but it may also mean that you win a fortune. This example also emphasizes the need to take into account the likelihood of any given outcome; losing is a great deal more likely that winning, in this particular case!

Where a decision results in significant losses for the client, carers may find themselves held responsible in law for these losses, especially if it is judged that the carers could readily have foreseen that such losses were likely. Although playing the Lottery may not arouse legal concerns, this issue can be particularly important, for example, in cases of people with learning disabilities who may offend sexually. The consequent loss of freedom which could result if the person is then legally detained could be considered to be the fault of the carers who did not take appropriate steps to contain the offending behaviour. In such cases, it is clear that a decision by carers to allow as much freedom and choice as possible for their client may need tempering with caution, and often require a careful balancing act between containing and enabling. It is worth bearing in mind that risk assessment needs to be a two-way process, including an assessment not only of risks to the person with learning disabilities, but also of any risks they may pose to others. Some people with learning disabilities will have a very vague sense of what is socially acceptable, or considered to be morally wrong.

Moral aspects of decisions and choices may be more difficult to convey to some people with learning disabilities. However, when choices are made about both general social and sexual behaviour it may be particularly important to ensure that the person concerned has some appreciation of what the moral, as well as the legal, implications of their choice are likely to be. Choosing to have sex with one's best friend's girlfriend may result in a number of unpleasant social repercussions, which are nothing to do with the sexual behaviour as such.

Similarly the wider social implications of choices may not be apparent to the person with learning disabilities, and it should be part of the responsibilities of care staff to ensure that their clients have some awareness of these implications. For example, choosing to wear unusual clothing, or to have an unusual hairstyle, while not necessarily undesirable in themselves, may make the person more vulnerable to teasing, rejection, bullying, or other forms of abuse. Limited experiences can mean that many people with learning disabilities do not understand the importance of such social rules and the risks that making such choices may present.

Problems often arise because the choices that people with learning disabilities make can embarrass others. Similarly, as above, the consequences of their choices may mean they embarrass themselves. Often they may not fully understand why their actions produced the result that they did, and as a consequence they become fearful of making further mistakes, and reluctant to take any chances. In these kinds of situation, care staff can help greatly by explaining afterwards, in simple terms, what went wrong and why. While this may not always solve the problem, sometimes it may help the person with learning disabilities to make better choices next time.

Protection versus Choice: Where to Draw the Line

For most growing children, parents make decisions about risks that affect their child in the same way as they make decisions for themselves. Having considered the risks involved in an activity, they put limits around the freedom their children have accordingly. As normal children grow, parents are constantly assessing the abilities of their children to cope with increasing levels of freedom and independence. Most parents, therefore, would allow a child of 13 to have greater freedom and take greater risks that they would a child of 5. Throughout their children's lives they take risks, and allow their children to take some limited risks. This is essential if the children are to gain the experiences which allow them to develop into normal adults.

As children develop, most parents relax rules, and allow the child more unsupervised activities and time away from them. This enables children to experiment and learn from their own mistakes, which is an essential part of becoming an adult. Most normal children take greater risks when they are away from their parents, and usually conceal this from them. What did you do as a child which you would never have dreamt of telling your parents about?

Most parents are aware that their children take risks, and generally they do not allow this to colour their decisions about what their children do to an unreasonable extent. We all know that the rate of teenage pregnancy is unacceptably high. However, the vast majority of us do not avoid that risk by locking up our teenage daughters. Instead we attempt to teach them about the risks they may run, and ensure they can deal with them appropriately, as far as possible.

People with learning disabilities, even when they have grown up at home, are often over-protected because of their difficulties and consequently do not have these opportunities for experimentation and learning. Their development tends not to follow the usual pattern, for both biological and social reasons, and this may result in them being treated as overgrown children for an extended period of their lives, and being given little opportunity to act independently or learn from their own mistakes, even as adults. For those who grow up in institutions such experiences and opportunities are even more limited, adding to their lack of ability to assess risk for themselves.

Sometimes choices are so complex that people with learning disabilities find it very difficult to understand what is involved, and this makes it impossible for them to make an informed choice. By 'informed choice' we mean that the person has assessed the likely implications and risks associated with the choice and still decided to make that choice. This is where the whole issue of 'consent' for people with learning disabilities becomes so complicated.

For example, consider the difficulty of a woman with learning disabilities making the decision to have a sexual relationship. First she has to understand what sex is, and what having sex with someone else involves at a physical level. She has to have some understanding of how sexual activity can lead to pregnancy, and she has therefore to understand what pregnancy is and how likely it is that she may become pregnant. Given this knowledge she has to know whether she wishes to become pregnant or not, and to do this she has to have some idea of what being pregnant will mean to her, and what it will mean to actually have a child. This may relate to her ability to physically give birth, or to how well she can care for the child, as well as the emotional implications of being a parent. There is also the risk that if she proves to be unable to care for the child it may be taken into care. In addition, having a child carries a number of legal and moral implications, as well as social and emotional ones.

If she is not to have the child, there are all the problems associated with making a decision about termination, including the likely physical, social and psychological repercussions of such a decision. Alternatively, she may decide to use contraception, and to do so she needs to know what is available, how it works, how to use it and what the medical risks associated with each kind may be. She may need to know that if she takes the 'morning after' pill this carries one set of risks, while the usual contraceptive pill carries other risks. If a physical barrier method is to be used for contraception, she or her partner must be able to learn how to use it effectively, to remember to use it, and have the physical dexterity to do so.

Once the decision to use contraception is made, then there are the moral considerations about sexual activity. Should people have sex outside marriage? What are the rules of her religion, if she has one? Is her partner's religion the same? What if one partner is already married, or already has a partner? How does the sexual relationship fit with other relationships? Where does 'love' come in the discussion? Is there any discussion, or has she simply been 'steamrollered' into a sexual relationship by a demanding partner? Is this the beginning of a long-term partnership, or a one-off, purely sexual encounter?

Then come all the health risks. Being pregnant and giving birth carry risks to health, as do certain contraceptive methods. The risk of contracting some kind of sexually transmitted disease is moderately high, even though the more serious risks like HIV infection may be still relatively low.

Ultimately, assuming that she has all this information available to her, and she can understand it, the woman then has to decide if all these risks are worth any pleasure she may gain from a sexual encounter. It is clear from all the above that making such a decision is a highly complex process, assuming that all of these things are adequately considered.

In fact, of course what actually happens is probably that, given the chance, she has sex with the man to whom she is attracted without much consideration of all the above. She takes a risk. How many women of normal ability take such a risk in exactly the same way, often many times in their lives? How many of them assess carefully all the risks described above? Is it fair that we should expect a higher standard of decision-making from people with learning disabilities that we demand from the majority of other people?

The difficulty that now exists for people with learning disabilities, especially those with greater handicaps, and those who care for and support them, is that the law specifies that many such people are vulnerable, and not able to make this choice for themselves. They are considered to be unable to assess the risks involved and thus make an independent choice. The onus of assessing risk and making the decision therefore often rests with carers. Because it is such a difficult decision to make for someone else, carers often take the simple way out, and avoid letting situations arise where learning-disabled people in their care have the opportunity to develop sexual relationships: if a person cannot make an 'informed choice' then perhaps it is easier not to offer them that choice. This is the current dilemma for those who work in community care situations. The issue of sexual relationships is perhaps the most difficult and complex, but this problem of balancing risk and choice is a constant one for carers and professionals, in relation to many aspects of everyday life. In the background is the ogre of the law (and/or local management), ready to jump on the unwary, should they get it wrong. No wonder, perhaps that many are cautious about enabling such choices to be made.

Summary

There are many risks to be considered in everyday life, which, as I have noted, we all take all the time. Because we have grown up with opportunities to make choices, take risks and weigh up the consequences, most of us give little thought to the process. A normal life is risky. Unfortunately, for many people with learning disabilities there have been far fewer opportunities to learn how to make choices, and in consequence far fewer opportunities to take risks and learn from their own mistakes. Parents and carers see the vulnerability of the person with learning disabilities and tend to consider the risks of everyday life as much higher than for someone without such a disability. In their fear of doing the wrong thing they deny the person the right to a truly 'normal life', which is, as for all of us, a risky one.

This book endeavours to look at the areas of life where risks are apparent, and to discuss to what extent these risks are real and signifi-cant. It aims to help you look at the lives of those in your care, whether your connection with them is personal or professional, and consider how you can use the process of risk assessment to enhance their lives rather than restrict them. 'Drawing the line' between choice and risk is not easy, but this book endeavours to help you make a decision based on a real assessment of the likely costs and benefits of each choice taken. It will suggest ways in which you can involve all interested parties in a decision-making system which can be clearly documented. If it is clear that a real attempt has been made to consider and document all possible outcomes, both negative and positive, and that a real consensus has been achieved, it is much less likely that carers or professionals will find themselves on the wrong side of the law. People with learning disabilities have been denied a normal life for far too long. It is hoped that this book will enable those who care for them to move further towards redressing the balance, without putting their clients in danger, or themselves at risk of prosecution.

chapter two

THE PROBLEM OF PREDICTING RISK

Understanding Risk

As outlined in chapter 1, the concept of risk is sometimes a difficult one. As we enter the new century, there is much talk in health and social service settings about 'risk assessment', but there seems to be much confusion about how this can realistically be done. Often it seems to deteriorate into the filling in of a form (the designated 'Risk Assessment Form') which is then filed, with a sigh of relief in the relevant client's file where it lies forgotten. Unless of course, someone asks whether risk assessments have been completed on all clients, when it can be taken out and waved around!

This may be an unduly cynical view, but there is no doubt that many people who work with people with learning disabilities feel anxious about the idea of doing 'risk assessments' and are rather vague about what they should entail. This book will attempt to demystify the process, and give professionals and carers a systematic approach to use in the process of risk assessment.

The first message about risk assessment, which must be taken on board by anyone who is serious about the process, is that *to be meaningful risk assessment must be ongoing*.

Let us consider a simple example. If you wish to cross a road, you will approach the edge of the pavement, and look for traffic. When you are sure that the road is clear, or that any traffic is far away enough for it to be safe to cross, you cross the road. Your decision-making process may be quite complex, in that you will watch the vehicles that are travelling on the road, make an assessment of their speed, and then judge how long it will take them to reach the place where you plan to cross. You will also make an assessment of your own speed, and how long it will take you to get across the road, and will compare this with your estimate of the vehicle's speed of approach before you decide whether to move or not. Thus the decision that it is safe to cross the road is a complex task, even though it may be completed in a matter of seconds.

Consider now if you approach the same road the next day, at the same time. Traffic conditions may be similar, and the amount of traffic may be much the same. How many of you would then cross the road without making any further assessment of the risk involved in doing so? It is more likely that you would repeat the assessment of the previous day, taking in to account the fact that today there are different vehicles on the road, perhaps travelling at different speeds. You may perhaps also need to consider that, for example, yesterday you sprained your ankle, so your own rate of movement will be correspondingly slower. A lot of everyday risks are of this kind. Situations change rapidly, and what applied yesterday may not apply today. Thus, to be useful and meaningful, many risk situations need to be reassessed regularly, perhaps daily. Filling in a form once in six months, or even once a month, is probably not enough, however carefully and thoroughly it is done. Decisions about risk-taking need to be regularly reviewed, even if a detailed reassessment of risk is not necessary.

To return to the example above, the initial assessment of the road and its traffic levels, together with an estimate of the length of time needed to cross the road, will all be essential pieces of information which contribute to the risk-taking decision. While these components may vary from day to day, some of the information will continue to be valid, and need not be reconsidered. The width of the road, the height of the kerb, and the distance at which the traffic can be seen, will probably not vary (although roadworks or bad weather might affect the latter), and estimates of risk on other days may be able to assume some constancy in these areas.

Assessments of other risks can follow the same pattern. A risk-assessment meeting, which has assessed all the areas of risk thoroughly, may not need to repeat the whole process: Some things will not have changed. However, it is important that assessments of risk are regularly reviewed: some things definitely *will* have changed. It is also important to evaluate any action that has been taken to reduce risk, and to assess whether this has worked. It may not have been possible to reduce the amount of traffic on our hypothetical road, but better training in road safety skills, or a new pair of glasses, may make the management of the risk much easier.

One of the many problems about assessing risk is that different people may perceive the level of risk differently. What is acceptable to one person or one community may not be acceptable to another. Objective assess-ment of risk, where it is possible, may affect decision-making in a number of ways. However, the reality is that most of us do not assess risk objectively, and our decision-making about risk is often flawed and strongly influenced by emotion and personal experience, as well as the amount of information that we have about the risk. This will be discussed in more detail later.

Risk versus Outcome

One of the difficulties about risk assessment is that much of the research literature has focused on the assessment of the risk of violence. Of course, violent people present a real hazard to others, but they present it in an unusual way. Even in habitually violent people, violence is a relatively low-rate behaviour, and it often occurs in quite specific situations. Therefore a great deal of work has been done to try to determine the kinds of conditions which may provoke violence, and to present those trying to manage and work with potentially violent people with the tools for predicting, and thus hopefully avoiding, such violence as far as possible. The main reason for this emphasis is the concern that violence and violent offending generates. The public are anxious for reassurance that they will not be put at risk of being victimized in such a way.

In fact these attempts at predicting violence have not been particularly successful, and the prediction of this kind of risk has been the focus of a large number of publications, many of which have stressed that it is an extremely difficult thing to do effectively. Certain factors, such as a past history of violence, are known to be fairly good predictors of future violence, but the reality is that people are complex systems, and any number of aspects of their behaviour can be affected by a variety of changes in the environment around them. It is not enough to label certain individuals as 'violent'. We all have a potential to be violent, but whether we actually become so will depend on what happens to us, and on the situations around us.

Often the factors which affect whether violence reoccurs or not are determined by chance events or a series of chance events occurring together. This is the most difficult aspect of risk assessment: many risks involve random elements which cannot be predicted and are not controllable. To return to our roadside scenario: a car may go out of control and leave the road, hitting us as we stand by the roadside contemplating the safe time to cross. This random aspect is usually very difficult, if not impossible, to predict, because of its low frequency of occurrence, and this makes any risk-assessment process extremely difficult.

Another reason that so much effort has gone into the prediction of violence is that the consequences of getting the answer wrong can be so disastrous. A child-killer may be released from custody with the prediction that he is unlikely to reoffend. Even if he goes on to kill only one child, this is a disaster for that child and its family. Understandably there is a public outcry, and everyone wants to be reassured that it won't happen again. Of course, in reality it is impossible to give this kind of assurance. There are too many variables in the equation to be able to be certain that such an offender will never do the same thing again. The only way to ensure such offenders do not reoffend is never to release any of them. Unfortunately this means that the institutions in which they are detained will have to increase in number considerably to accommodate them all. It also means that many people who would not reoffend will be locked up unnecessarily. Some people would advocate the use of the death penalty as a solution to the problem, but because criminal justice systems are fallible, some innocent people would probably also be killed, and many people feel that this is not an acceptable or humane solution in modern times.

Although most of the risks that are considered in this book are not related to this kind of serious violence, there is a theme here that can be of value. This is the second important factor in the assessment of risk. *The seriousness of the possible outcome of taking a risk must be balanced against the benefits of taking that risk.* This also highlights the point that not all risk-taking is necessarily a bad thing. Risk-taking can have positive as well as negative outcomes.

For example, if someone with a learning disability wishes to go to the local shops alone, this can be both important and valuable as an experience. The person will gain a sense of independence, will feel less controlled by others, will have a chance to learn about the use of money, how to find their way around, and will be able to make real choices about what to buy. They may meet new people, see new things, and gain in confidence as a result of this experience. Each time they do this, they will become more confident in their abilities to cope with everyday activities alone, and to make choices about how they spend their time. Such risk-taking promotes learning and psychological and emotional growth.

However, there will be a number of risks to consider. They may get run over by a car. They may lose their money, or be robbed. They may be exploited by an unscrupulous shopkeeper, or sexually assaulted as they walk to or from the shop. They may fall over and break a leg, have a fit, or faint, or be savaged by a dog. They may forget the way to the shop, or how to get home, or simply forget the time, and wander off somewhere else. None of these outcomes is particularly desirable. However, it also has to be acknowledged that all of them could apply to almost all of us at some time in our lives. In reality, of course, what usually happens is that we walk to the shop, buy what we want, and come home again. The same is true for many people with learning disabilities. The problem is that we are often much more likely, it seems, to foresee these disasters happening to others than we are to see them happening to ourselves.

This brings us to the next consideration in assessing risk. *How likely is it that this particular outcome will happen?*

In practice, of course, it is often extremely difficult to predict accurately what are likely outcomes and what are not. We do not always have accurate information on which to base our decisions. Our assessment of risk is coloured by our own experiences and those of our friends and family, or by stories in the media. These may lead us to overestimate dangers, and underestimate benefits. As discussed previously, previous exposure to information about a danger, or personal experience of a negative outcome, is likely to lead us to overestimate the chance of a negative outcome for our client.

Of significant importance is the information we already have about the person who is taking the risk. If, for example, the person going to the shop is very forgetful in everyday life, often loses things or gets lost, then we may rightly assume that the risk of something of this kind going wrong may be higher for that person. These kinds of risk factors will usually be well known to families or carers, as will a tendency to fits or fainting. The problem is that because of their concerns, and the difficulty of accurately predicting risk, both they and we may overestimate the likelihood of problems occurring, and thus prevent the person from having those experiences. Where the concerns are real, and the client is genuinely felt to be at risk because of such difficulties, it is important for care staff or families to try and be creative in enabling as much choice as possible, while still offering care and protection. The real challenge is to determine how accurate our estimates of negative outcome actually are.

As stated above, recent experiences or information can distort our assessment of risk, and we may overestimate a risk simply because it has come to our attention recently. An extreme example of this is when someone has been a victim of rape. For some considerable time after the rape, that person tends to overestimate the risk that rape will happen again, and remains excessively fearful, often refusing to go out alone, and avoiding places or people who provoke memories of the attacker. The same effect can occur, although to a lesser degree, if the unpleasant experience has happened to a friend or relative: we may see the likelihood of a negative outcome as being higher than objective measures would suggest it actually is.

It is well known that the media are often to blame for increasing people's estimates of risk in certain situations. It has been found that elderly people, especially women living alone, tend to overestimate their risk of being a victim of violent crime. In fact, statistics show that elderly women are the least likely to be victims of such crimes. The most likely victims of violent crime are in fact young men, who get into arguments and fights with each other, often after drinking alcohol. Likewise, the risk of being a murder victim is still relatively low in the UK, although it may be somewhat higher in the USA. However, the emphasis on murder in the reporting of crime in the media may lead one to assume that murderers lurk around every corner.

The likelihood of being a victim of a violent crime, or of being run over, for example, will also depend on factors such as the area in which a person lives. Some urban areas are more likely to be associated with such events than others. Rural areas tend to be safer generally. If we know the shopkeepers, and the local area, we will be in a better position to make a reasonable assessment of how likely it is that a person will be victimized on their way to the shop, or after they get there.

As mentioned above, what no one can predict very effectively is what might be called the 'random element'. As in our road-crossing example, a car may go out of control because the driver falls asleep at the wheel, and, as a result, three pedestrians are killed, one of which is our client. Once again, however, we have to ask ourselves how likely this is to occur. Statistically it is probably not very likely. More importantly, our client with learning disabilities is no more at risk from this kind of danger than we are ourselves. We do not hesitate to go outside or walk along the street because of the risk of such events, so it seems unreasonable to prevent our clients from doing so.

It is therefore important to separate out the elements of risk which are directly associated with the client's disabilities, and those which have a random and uncontrollable dimension, to which we are all subject.

Personal Choices about Risk

As already discussed, almost every activity carries an element of risk, and one of the most important ways in which we assess risk for ourselves is by considering the possible outcome. Where this is particularly unpleasant, for example the risk that we might contract AIDS, CJD, or lung cancer, we may find the prospect is enough to discourage us from taking the risk at all. However, in reality many common activities carry a short-term benefit which, for many people, outweighs the longer-term risk. The thrill of having sex with a new partner may outweigh the risk of contracting HIV or AIDS. The enjoyment of a good piece of roast beef may outweigh the risk of developing CJD at some later stage. The pleasure and relaxation associated with smoking may make the risk of lung cancer seem less important.

Each of these activities presents a fairly certain immediate reward, while the long-term risk seems much more remote and uncertain, and therefore unlikely. It is fairly certain I will enjoy the sex, the roast beef, or the cigarette. It is far from certain that I will contract the unpleasant illness with which each of these activities may be associated. This means that there is a tendency in most of us to play down the long-term risks where the likelihood of an unpleasant outcome seems fairly remote, the immediate pleasure is significant, and a degree of egocentricity leads us to believe that 'it won't happen to me'.

This conflict between short-term gain and long-term cost is a constant problem for those involved in health education. Most of us are much more readily influenced by short-term gain, and less likely to accept that the risks apply to us. The level of risk has to be quite high before the majority of people consider that the short-term gain is not worth the long-term cost. This is where personal experience may again be influential; if one had seen a friend die of lung cancer, this may have a much more powerful effect on one's behaviour than any amount of written information. The level of risk has not changed, of course, but the impact of personal experience and the emotions associated with that frequently influence decision-making much more powerfully than anything else.

So choices about whether or not to take risks for ourselves are often more influenced by emotion and experience than objective assessment of the real level of risk. You may feel that the pleasure and relaxation that you gain from smoking makes the risk of possible health problems worth taking. I may feel that eating a lot of chocolate is worth the risk of gaining a lot of weight, and possibly developing diabetes or heart problems as a consequence. Each of us will have a different opinion as to what risks are acceptable, what pleasures are important, and also *what we perceive the level of risk to be.* As a rule, we cannot and should not make these choices for someone else. Sometimes our choices or decisions about risk may seem stupid to others, but we do not feel that this gives them the right to stop us from making our personal choice. Most people would feel extremely resentful and angry if others tried to tell them what to eat, or whether they could smoke or have sex with someone else. Yet this is what happens for many people with learning disabilities.

The difficulty for people with learning disabilities is that carers often do feel that they are expected to make these choices for them. Their concern about keeping their clients safe tends to overrule those clients' freedom of choice, because they see those choices as unwise and associated with a high level of risk. It is interesting that there seems to be a much greater inclination to overestimate the risks that apply to others. This may be because we are not then directly influenced by the attraction of the short-term gains, but is probably also because carers and professionals are frequently concerned that they may be held responsible if things do go wrong. As mentioned before, the law of negligence can appear to inhibit decision-making. Personal freedom and choice sit uncomfortably next to the concepts of duty of care and professional liability.

However, there is no logical reason why people with learning disabilities should not make their own decisions and choices, as far as they are able to. At times they will make mistakes, and the outcome will not be what they had wanted. The same is true for most of us, and indeed this is often the way that we learn what we want, and how to make better choices in the future. Making a mistake means that one has not yet discovered the right way to do something, and this applies to making choices and decisions too. Most of us have had opportunities to learn how to do this as we have grown up. People with learning disabilities may not have done. Perhaps carers need to be encouraged to help their clients learn how to make choices with an appreciation of the risks involved. This is a much more challenging task than just encouraging choice alone.

Thus it would seem that not only should people with learning disabilities be allowed to make choices and take risks, *they should actively be encouraged to do so*. Like the growing child, it is only by having such experiences, and making mistakes, that they will learn how to do it better in the future. It could be argued that excessive protection of people with learning disabilities is actually contravening the Human Rights Act, by depriving them of certain basic choices and freedoms. Unfortunately, the demands of other pieces of legislation may conflict with this requirement, and this may only be resolved by particular cases being fought in court. Most of us do not relish the prospect of being involved with one of those test cases.

A Duty of Care

The problem with the right to make choices is that it assumes that people with learning disabilities are able to make choices about risk in the same way that everyone does. Of course, in many areas of life clients may be able to make choices readily, especially if these are relatively simple. Nevertheless, we have to acknowledge that people with learning disabilities do have real difficulties with many cognitive tasks. Thus, if most us have problems in assessing risk effectively because of the complexity of doing so it is likely that people with learning disabilities will find the task particularly difficult. It may therefore be that, rather than giving them opportunities to learn and grow, we are simply overloading them – demanding more from them than they are capable of giving. People with learning disabilities often have problems in coping with everyday activities and, as I have stressed, those of us who work with such clients do have a duty of care. Where clients really cannot cope with the demands that life is placing on them, it is essential that carers support and protect them. How can the right path be found between such apparently conflicting legal requirements?

There is a large overlap here with the assessment of ability to consent and the ability to make real choice, especially in relation to understanding the likely consequences of the choice or decision made. It may be helpful when trying to make any assessment of this capacity to consider the following:

- Is the person aware that a decision or choice can be made, and what that is?
- Are they aware that there may be more than one option?
- Do they understand what may happen as a result of each possible choice?
- Do they appreciate that some of these results may cause harm to themselves or others?
- Can they communicate a choice?
- Can they be helped in any way to make and communicate a choice?

Giving people with learning disabilities more choice, especially about taking risks, does mean that we have to be alert to the extent to which the client is able realistically to assess the level of risk involved. A person with severe learning disabilities, who has little language, cannot be said to be making a real choice if he or she decides to wander down the middle of a busy street. It is very unlikely that this person has a real understanding of the risks involved in walking amongst traffic, or the likely outcomes. In such a situation a court would probably judge that the risk had been taken by the failure to act, and carers would be seen as being negligent as result of an act of *omission*, not *commission*.

In these kinds of cases, we would usually accept that we have a duty of care to keep the person physically safe, regardless of their expressed choice. This could be achieved in a number of ways, for example by confining them to their home or by accompanying them as they take their walk. The latter, of course, gives the person with learning disabilities some choice and independence, and more real freedom. Our role as carers and professionals carries the responsibility to consider the best interests of our clients. Does the duty of care mean that we should prevent someone from taking a risk, or does it mean that we should look at more creative ways of trying to ensure their safety while allowing as much choice as possible?

This is where decision-making becomes difficult for carers. In order to decide when a risk is acceptable, they need to consider a large number of pieces of information. They must then weigh these against each other, all the while being aware that their employers, the client's family, and the public at large, are likely to hold them responsible if things go wrong. In addition, many services remain understaffed and personnel are stressed. This does not encourage creative problem-solving. If people with learning disabilities are to improve their quality of life, and be allowed to experience 'real life' with all its attendant hazards and risks, carers and other professionals need to have the time and resources to do their jobs properly. There need to be enough staff for clients to be able to have one-to-one attention if that is what is necessary for them to have such choices, and the role, pay and level of qualification of such staff may need to be reviewed.

Currently care staff are often forced to take the most restrictive path because their lack of resources makes any other choice impossible. It is often in the context of such an unsatisfactory situation that they are also required to undertake 'risk assessments' with the uncomfortable awareness that they will be held responsible for any untoward consequences. No wonder that many staff play safe and limit the chances that their clients have to take risks.

Assessing risk on behalf of others is a task fraught with problems. Above all else the chief requirement is for information. It is impossible to assess risk of any kind without a detailed history of the individual and a real understanding of the level of risk attached to each activity under consideration. However, attention also needs to be given to the working environment (and its prevailing attitudes) in which such assessments are taking place. If staff feel that they will always be held to blame for untoward consequences of risk-taking by their clients, they will inevitably play safe and thereby limit the life choices and experiences of their learning-disabled clients. There has to be a willingness amongst managers to create a climate where risk-taking is acceptable as long as all involved have discussed and agreed the process and considered all possible outcomes, including what will be gained by taking the risk, as well as what could go disastrously wrong. Furthermore, staffing levels need to be adequate for staff to be able to actively engage in work with clients. If there are only enough staff to cope with basic activities such as cooking, cleaning and shopping, then there will be little opportunity to develop sophisticated skills such as decision-making and assessing risks.

Assessing risk and making choices about those risks means that staff groups need to consider (among other things) the following questions:

1 What are the likely outcomes of taking this risk?
2 How likely is it that any given outcome will happen, if the risk is taken?
3 Is the outcome so serious that the risk cannot be countenanced?
4 Can any action be taken to reduce the impact of the outcome if problems do occur?
5 What will the person gain from the experience that requires this risk to be taken?
6 How likely is it that this experience will be useful or pleasurable to the person?
7 Does the likelihood of harm outweigh the likelihood of benefit?
8 What would I choose for myself, or for members of my family?
9 What do colleagues feel that they would choose?
10 How much awareness of the likely risks and outcomes does the client have?
11 Can this client weigh up the costs and benefits of this particular decision about risk?
12 If not, is there a consensus about what should be done among those who know the client well?

In the course of discussing the above questions, ideas will be generated about the risks being taken, and how these can be minimized. Ideally this should be a group discussion and a group decision, including family members if at all possible. The progress of such a meeting could be recorded on some kind of risk-assessment form, although, as discussed earlier, these tend to have significant limitations if they become an end in themselves. It is the process, not the form, which is important.

It is also wise to avoid assessing risk by assigning numerical values to different levels of risk. Although this is often done, it can be misleading and even dangerous. It tends to give a false air of scientific validity to what is produced in writing. It is much wiser to restrict the decision-making process to a verbal and written assessment of the levels of risk as agreed (and, if necessary, researched) by all concerned.

Nevertheless, it is often helpful to have an ordered framework within which to work, and a means of recording the process. The next chapter will consider the factors that contribute to risk for the individual, and then go on to examine such a framework, together with examples to illustrate how to use it, in order to help answer the above questions.

Summary

Assessing risk is a complex process, yet it is one which we are all engaged in, all the time. There seems to be a tendency to underestimate risk for ourselves, while overestimating it for those in our care. This puts parents and care staff in a difficult position, and the tendency in the past has been to limit and control the person with learning disabilities, rather than encouraging them to make their own decisions as far as possible. The overall effect of this approach has been that people with learning disabilities have been denied to right to make even the most basic decisions about their lives. This seems at best unfair, and at worst abusive.

Assessing and managing risk inevitably raises questions about the client's ability to consent, and the extent to which they should be enabled to make their own choices and decisions. While this is, or should be, the ideal to which we aspire, in practice it is important to balance the responsibility for a duty of care against the desire to allow an individual as much freedom as possible. In assessing risk, it may well become apparent that an assessment of intellectual capacity is necessary in order to decide on the best and safest course of action.

Those making decisions about risks also need to be aware that they will have their own agenda about what is right and wrong, and that it may not be appropriate to impose their own feelings on decisions about other people's lives. This is why taking decisions about risk management is best done by a group of interested and responsible individuals rather than one person. Nor does it seem fair to insist that people with learning disabilities should have to assess risks to a level of detail and complexity that nobody else does. We should allow them to choose to take risks at least some of the time, just as the rest of us do, as long as we are not failing in our duty of care. In order to try and get the balance right, it is helpful to have a structured approach to risk assessment, and the next chapter will attempt to provide a framework which can be helpful in addressing the problems of assessing and managing risks.

chapter three

ASSESSING RISKS AND ESTABLISHING CARE PLANS

Assessing Risk to Self and Others: Looking at Past Behaviour

People who regularly indulge in risky or dangerous behaviour often have a history of doing so. The more long-standing and extensive this history is, the more likely it is that they will indulge in such behaviour again. This is true whether the risk-taking appears to be deliberate, and the result of active choice, such as excessive use of alcohol, or whether it appears to be accidental, such as leaving the gas cooker on by mistake. It is also true of violent or aggressive behaviour. It is often said that the best predictor of future behaviour is past behaviour. This is particularly true of violence, and it applies equally to people with or without learning disabilities.

A history of sexually inappropriate or offending behaviour is particularly worrying. Even if the person concerned has not been involved in sexual misdemeanours for some years it does not mean that their potential for such behaviour is diminished. This can remain the case, even when the person has received treatment. Treatment of sex offenders is notoriously difficult and time-consuming, and has a high relapse rate. Even where there has been no formal conviction, which is common for people with learning disabilities, it is foolhardy to assume that sexually motivated, undesirable behaviours are easily changed. Sexual urges are often strong and recurring, and consequently are a powerful motivating force, tending to maintain any behaviour which results in sexual satisfaction. Even with intensive treatment and good motivation on the part of the 'offender' it is difficult to change sexual behaviour. If there has been *no* treatment intervention, then it is very unlikely that the potential for sexually inappropriate behaviour will have disappeared spontaneously, even when environmental factors may have suppressed it for many years.

Sexually inappropriate behaviour usually has its roots in early experiences, especially of sexual abuse, and such problems tend to be quite resistant to change. With many learning-disabled people the most successful way to avoid further problems is by effective management. When the person concerned may have been living in a setting where the opportunities for such behaviour have been very limited or absent, carers and professionals are sometimes tempted to assume that because the recent past has been incident-free the problem has disappeared. *This is extremely unlikely.*

The same is true when the person has been living in an environment where a behavioural programme has been in operation for some time, and this programme has addressed a particular behavioural problem. If the programme has been successful, the behaviour may not have been recorded for some considerable time. However, this does not mean that the problem has disappeared. Given the right (or wrong!) conditions, it may well re-emerge. This is particularly true of certain types of challenging behaviour.

It is also important to consider other historical factors. The presence or absence of particular people, situations, demands, or stimuli can all affect the likelihood of certain types of behaviour which may have contributed to risk for that individual. Self-injury, for example, may be triggered by such situations as being subject to too many demands, being bored, being depressed, or being angry and frustrated. Keeping the person with learning disabilities safe may mean ensuring that their environment is structured in a particular way so that the chances of the above are minimized. It may be necessary to spend some time looking at the context and conditions which surround any problem behaviour. Risks associated with self-harm or violence, for example, can often be minimized by appropriate management of these factors. It may be helpful to seek the help of a clinical psychologist to assist in establishing appropriate management strategies for these kinds of behaviour, and thereby minimizing risk. It must be accepted that it will take time to collect all the relevant information about the person who is being assessed, including personal history, as well as current environmental factors that may influence their present behaviour patterns.

In all cases, it will be helpful where possible to access information about past problems, treatment interventions, drug history, family history, and current contacts. Previous homes, hospitals, families and day-care centres or work placements can often provide useful information. It is not unusual to find that different settings will have different views about the individual: different environments can produce different behaviour. It is important to remember during this stage that an absence of information does not mean an absence of risk. While it is important not to allow negative perceptions of the person to damn them out of hand, it is also important to listen to previous carers and others involved with the client, and consider carefully the information offered. *Read reports which are in the client's files.* They have been put there for a reason, and will often offer ideas and strategies for minimizing risk both to the client and others. Staff often take unnecessary risks because past information is not made available to them, or because they choose not to take the time to read files, reports, etc.

Where the client has a history of violent offending towards others, including sexual offending, it is particularly important to obtain information about past offences. It is likely that there will be patterns of behaviour associated with them. The person may only offend in certain settings, or may choose a particular type of victim. Some offenders will only offend if they are mentally ill, or drunk, or have taken drugs. It may be possible to minimize the risk of reoffending by controlling these aspects of their life.

People with learning disabilities are less likely to have a history of formally documented offences. Police and the courts tend to take a more lenient view, and it is not uncommon to find men with learning disabilities who have been 'offending' sexually for years without any real sanctions having been applied. Usually this is because they have been living in environments where they were able to target weaker or less able fellow clients and exploit them sexually. Sometimes it will be because staff, especially female carers, have just 'put up with' inappropriate sexually motivated behaviour which, if it had occurred in another setting, they would clearly have defined as sexual assault.

Unfortunately, this failure to document such behaviour or to impose sanctions on the people who are responsible for it can result in serious repercussions when they move into more community-based settings. Previously tolerated behaviour, which has not been defined as unacceptable or assaultative, can bring the learning-disabled 'offender' into serious conflict with the law, or it may just cause problems with local people. For example, it is by no means unknown for local people to take exception to such behaviour and to demonstrate this by means of violent retribution. A learning-disabled 'offender' may find himself the target of ostracism, name-calling, or even violence when local communities become aware of his sexually inappropriate behaviour. The law may be lenient, but the community may not.

It is clearly not in the interests of anyone in this situation for the person with learning disabilities to be allowed to continue in this kind of behaviour. The assessment of risk here must include an assessment of the risks to both the community and to the 'offender' himself. These issues will be considered in more depth in later chapters.

Other Factors that Affect Risk

As suggested above, a history of mental illness, drug-taking, or excessive alcohol use, may each be associated with an increase in certain types of risk. Ageing and the possible onset of dementia can also pose risks to the client or to those with whom he or she lives. Even if these are only suspected, it may be important to alert others to the possibility of their existence, as they can often affect the prediction of risk quite significantly. This can be risk to the client or to others, and may often be both.

A history of physical abuse in early life is often associated with aggressive or violent behaviour in adult life. In people with learning disabilities, this will often have been labelled as 'challenging behaviour'. Sometimes the behaviour has developed as an attempt to communicate distress. Sometimes it is simply a safety measure – a way of keeping others at a distance. Cultural factors will affect it, as will the kind of response that it receives. Where carers fail to understand the function of the aggression or violence, it may well become entrenched as a maladaptive response to what is seen as a hostile world.

Similarly a history of sexual abuse will often be associated with later sexual offending or sexually inappropriate behaviour. Certain types of self-injury and drug or alcohol abuse can also be associated with a history of sexual abuse, although these patterns are less often seen in people with learning disabilities. In assessing risk, it is very important in all cases to try and gain some understanding of the function of the behaviour – why does the person do it?

A history of a head injury, or a difficult birth, may be relevant in explaining past or current difficulties which the person experiences. Even a relatively mild head injury can lead to problems of memory and concentration, which may result in the person being more of a risk to themselves and/or others. Any kind of brain injury can result in epilepsy, which carries its own risks, and people with learning disabilities tend to be more prone to epilepsy. This may result in a higher than average level of risk to health from falls, etc., and can make it particularly difficult for carers to feel confident in promoting independence for these clients.

All these additional factors are discussed in more detail later, as they all have implications for care which add complexity to the assessment of risk. Serious risks are, perhaps, less often encountered in the average community home, and many of the concerns that care staff have centre around more day-to-day activities. However, it should be remembered that the early history of many people with learning disabilities who currently live in the community has often included periods of time in institutional care. Often they were admitted to this care while still very young, and the emotional impact of this must have been significant. It is also clear from the testimony of some of the more able of these people that this type of care was distressingly often associated with both physical and sexual abuse. Although such abuse may be long past, its effects will linger, and many of the behavioural problems encountered in people with learning disabilities can have their roots in these early experiences. Where clients are able to make choices about risk, their own choices may be coloured by such experiences, and their psychological reactions to their experiences, in addition to possible mental disorder, may result in excessively risky behaviours, such as promiscuity, self-injury, or even suicide attempts. Often apparently odd behaviours, such as food hoarding, have their roots in the deprivation experienced in institutional care.

Whatever the type and level of risk to be assessed, the process can follow a similar pattern. The process needs to be systematic and based on good-quality information, both about clients themselves and about the proposed choice or activity which is seen as posing the risk. It is worth spending time examining how the process can be developed, and how decisions can be made and communicated.

Weighting Decisions and Weighty Decisions

Life is about taking risks, and it is not realistic to imagine that risks can be totally avoided. However, some risks carry more serious consequences than others, and it is often the likely consequence of taking a risk which helps us to decide whether to take that risk or not. If the consequence of the risk will affect both the individual and those around him or her, then this tends to be viewed as more serious than when the risk-taking individual is the only person affected.

However, the problem when considering people with learning disabilities, as already highlighted, is that those making the decisions about risk are often concerned that they will be held responsible if things go wrong. In a climate that is critical and unsupportive, care staff are likely to be super-cautious, and thus somewhat restrictive of their clients' freedom.

As can be seen from the outlines above, there are a wide range of factors to be considered when assessing these kinds of risks, and good-quality information about the client and their situation is vital to good risk assessment. Even then it needs to be acknowledged by all involved in the process that taking a risk allows for the possibility that harm will follow. Risks can be considered at a number of levels and this may help in the decision-making process. The most serious risks involve possible death or injury, either to the client or to others. Other risks may be of exploitation, embarrassment, or distress. Sometimes, as with the risk of pregnancy, there are multiple risks that may follow from a single decision to engage in sexual activity. Where medical decisions are involved there is the problem that a medical intervention may in itself be risky, but may also carry consequences which the client may not foresee or understand. An example here might be the decision to be sterilized, which may be later regretted if a new partnership is established.

Ideally to evaluate risk one has to know what the real likelihood is that any undesirable consequence will happen following a given action. If this is, say, 1 in 2, then most people would agree that the risk is high and probably should not be taken: it is as likely that things will go wrong as not. If, however, the risk were 1 in 1,000, then most people would probably agree that it is a relatively low risk, and perhaps would take a chance. This is where the unpleasantness of the outcome becomes more significant. If the risk is of death, then 1 in 1,000 may still be too great a likelihood to take the chance. If the risk is of getting lost, then it is probably an acceptable level of risk.

The problem is that the difficulty of obtaining reliable estimates of the likelihood of any given outcome may be considerable. Even where the estimate is thought to be accurate, if other people feel able to take the risk, then is it right to restrict the opportunities of a learning-disabled person to do so, if they wish? Once again, the outcome of taking the risk may determine the decision. If the outcome will affect others, or it is felt that the person with learning disabilities is unable to assess the level of risk for him- or herself, then others will probably feel that they should intervene and prevent the client from taking the risk.

There are therefore a number of different aspects of risk to consider:

- *Nature of the risk to the client*
- *Risk to others*
- *Frequency of risky activity* – how often the activity occurs
- *Level of risk* – likelihood of undesirable outcome
- *Possible outcomes* – including short- and long-term, and good and bad. (Who will be affected? How important is this outcome?)

All risk assessment needs to consider risk in each of these ways, which inevitably interact with each other. An activity which carries a risk of a highly undesirable outcome may still be considered worthwhile if it is not very frequently undertaken, and the level of risk is low. For many people, flying in an aeroplane might come into this category.

It is clear that an activity which is undertaken frequently, where the person is at high risk of things going wrong, and where the outcome is possible death would be a highly risky activity. Even where the likely outcome is not death, if there is a serious risk of harm, and long-term risks as well, then the activity will be considered high-risk. However it is assessed, it is important to consider all aspects of any risky situation, including the likely positive outcomes from taking a risk.

Some approaches to risk assessment attempt to apply ratings or numbers to their estimates of risk. The difficulty in trying to apply numbers or formulas to the process is that people tend to rely too heavily on them, and cease to use their common sense. In reality, there is rarely a clear line between a risk which is acceptable and one which is unacceptable, and if figures are used, the 'cut off' may become an arbitrary figure which bears little relationship to actual experience. The danger is that by applying numbers one may appear to be giving the assessment a false air of scientific accuracy, which is not justified.

Ultimately there is no substitute for knowing your client well, and making a judgement based on a consensus of opinion from a number of people who also know him or her well. The problem is that emotions, moral judgements and personal experience can often influence such judgements. It is important that anyone involved in risk assessment is aware of this possibility, and can ensure that the risk picture is not unduly distorted by one opinion. Thus it is always useful and important to get more than one opinion.

What Will Happen if You Are Wrong?

Taking a risk implies an acceptance of the possibility that things will go wrong, and that the undesirable outcome will occur. The essence of risk assessment is to try and minimize that likelihood if possible. However, it does also implicitly accept that *sometimes things will go wrong.* It is also important to recognize that some risks are more controllable than others. The risk of being hit by lightning is low, but largely uncontrollable; the risk of being run over by a car is higher, but somewhat more controllable, in that care can be taken in crossing roads. However, even here there is a random element: a drunken hit and run driver or a car careering out of control can kill even the most careful pedestrian.

Often the choice to take a risk is driven by the attraction of a positive outcome. The possible negative outcome tends to be played down. The likelihood of the alternatives needs to be considered. If the gains achieved by taking the risk are seen as great enough, then most people will take the risk and hope the negative outcome does not occur. However, if it does, it is important that everyone involved in making the decision accepts that *the negative outcome can happen*, and has a strategy for dealing with it when it does.

At times, when a strategy can be identified, it may be felt that this makes taking a risk less worrying. It is vital that when risk assessments are carried out all possible outcomes are considered, and that a consensus is obtained from all those involved that the proposed course of action, and associated risk, is acceptable.

Recording Risks and Making Decisions

When it is clear that the client is unable to assess risk for themselves, and that others need to make this assessment on their behalf, it is important to have a process for doing so. This should not rely solely on the completion of a standard form, and ideally should not be carried out by one person alone. Where risks are to be taken, it is important that all who are involved regularly in the care of the client are involved in the decision-making process.

This may sound unwieldy, but it need not be. Where clients live in community homes, all that is required is that all staff involved in the care of the person have an opportunity to agree what is acceptable and what is not. A meeting may be necessary to do this, and this could be incorporated into a regular review meeting. When other professionals are not involved, it may only be necessary to gain a consensus between care staff. Whatever the process, the decision should be recorded formally, in writing, and placed in the client's file. This document should be signed and dated, and include an account of the risk to be taken, the likely benefits, and an estimate of the likelihood of the unwanted outcome. However, what is crucial is that all staff involved in the care of the client should be made aware of the existence of this decision. This should apply to agency and other temporary staff also. Where the client has regular contact with other professionals, such as the GP, social worker, or a clinical psychologist, and where parents or other family members are regularly involved, then these people should also be included in the risk-assessment process.

Let us examine a risk-assessment process for a typical person with learning disabilities.

MARY

Mary lives in a community home with three other residents. Mary has little language, but understands much of what is said to her. Mary enjoys going shopping and frequently walks to the local shop to buy sweets, biscuits and soft drinks. She may do this two or three times a day if no one intervenes. Mary is 29 years of age, and has no experience of sexual relationships. However, she likes being with people, especially men, and can seem flirtatious in her behaviour. Mary has recently acquired a new keyworker, a young man who has just joined the staff of the home. He expresses concern to the home manager about the risks posed by Mary's behaviour.

The home manager should respond quickly to this new member of staff's concerns. There are a number of possible risks here which need to be considered. The outline below suggests a strategy for the home manager to follow.

Assessment of risks

RISKS TO MARY

1 *Contact all involved in Mary's care to attend a risk-assessment meeting*
These include Mary's mother, her care manager, and all staff who look after her at the home (four other people). The first practical problem is that Mary's mother works full-time, and not all staff can attend a meeting at once, because other residents need to be supervised as well. To accommodate Mary's mother the meeting might be held in the early evening. To obtain input from the whole staff team, a mechanism needs to be put in place to obtain views from each person. Perhaps after the initial meeting, when the risks have been identified, those not present at the meeting could be asked by the home manager to make an indi-

vidual assessment on the risks identified. The final decision could be made by the home manager after collating all opinions, and communicated in writing to all interested parties, together with the reasons for making the decision. As with child protection conferences, all involved should be asked to make a judgement, and the majority view should hold sway. In the case of a split decision the home manager might hold the casting vote, or it may be considered more appropriate to give it to Mary's mother, or to a care manager. This enables any risk-taking to be a joint and shared responsibility, after detailed analysis of the risks involved.

Where there is involvement of social services, the responsibility for co-ordinating risk assessments may be seen to lie with them. While this may be true in law, there is nothing to stop other professional and/or care staff from developing their own procedures, either with the co-operation of social services staff or without them. Ultimately the buck will stop with those who are responsible for the care of the people with learning disabilities, and in carrying out good risk assessments they are protecting both their clients' interests and their own.

2   *At the risk-assessment meeting all possible risks should be identified and recorded*

(a)   The risk of leaving the house alone
   • How good is Mary's road sense?
   • Is she at risk of being run over?
   • Will she wander off or get lost?

(b)   The risk of being exploited
   • Mary has little language. She may not understand what is said to her.
   • Does she have any understanding of money?
   • How does she pay for her purchases? Is the shopkeeper treating her fairly?
   • Are there likely to be others around the shops who might steal from her?

(c)   The risk of being sexually victimized
   • Mary appears to like men. Would she go off with someone she did not know?
   • How good is her knowledge of sex?
   • Does she appear to be sexually aware?

- Is her flirtatious behaviour such that she might appear to invite sexual contact?

(d)   The risk to her health
  - Mary likes to buy sweets, biscuits and soft drinks.
  - If she is doing this every day, or even two or three times a day, she is at risk of gaining weight, and suffering from dental decay.

3   *Having identified the nature of the risks, consider how likely it is that Mary is at risk*

(a)   *The risk of leaving the house alone.* Mary has been walking to the local shops for several years. The road she walks along is quiet, and the shops are at the end. Mary has never attempted to cross the road alone, and she has never been known to wander off alone. Past knowledge of Mary therefore suggests that although she may not have much road sense, she does not attempt to cross roads alone, nor to leave her familiar route. The road she walks along is well known to her. If Mary of continues her present behaviour she is unlikely to be at serious risk of harm from leaving home. However, it should be borne in mind that any change in the nature of the road, or Mary's behaviour, could change this risk greatly. On the positive side, Mary probably gains a sense of independence and freedom from her opportunity to go out alone and purchase what she wants.

(b)   *The risk of being exploited.* Mary has been visiting these local shops for years. She buys what she wants by picking up her choices and offering the shopkeeper one or more pound coins to cover the cost of her purchases. They tell her how many they need from her and give her the change. Mary is well known to the local shopkeepers, and she is well treated by them. The area is quiet and most of the other customers are elderly. The shopkeepers would be likely to intervene if they saw Mary being exploited by anyone. The situation would be very different if the shops were in a busy housing estate, with a lot of youngsters hanging around them. The risk would also be considerably greater if Mary was not known to the shopkeepers, or if the shop changed hands.

(c)   *The risk of being sexually victimized.* Mary appears to like men, but she is actually quite selective in whom she approaches. She likes to spend time with the male residents in her home, and sits close to them at home, for example when watching TV. She giggles and will cuddle up to men she knows well, such as fellow residents or male members of staff.

However, she is much more wary of people she does not know. Nevertheless, it does not take long for Mary to lose her shyness, and she already tries to cuddle her new keyworker.

Mary could be at risk of sexual victimization if someone took the time to get to 'know' her first, e.g. by meeting regularly with her when she makes her visits to the shops, and building up a sense of familiarity and trust. Otherwise she is probably not at any greater risk than any other woman is.

(d)   *The risk to her health.* Mary may go out to the shops two or three times a day if not supervised. She has gained about half a stone in weight over the last year, and on her last visit to the dentist she had to have three fillings. It is clear that Mary's habits of buying sweets, biscuits and drinks are beginning to have an undesirable effect on her health. If left unchecked these changes could become a more serious problem. However, Mary has few hobbies and these shopping trips and the items that she buys are a source of great pleasure to her.

Risks to others

Mary is not a risk to others.

Having discussed the four main areas of risk for Mary, it is clear that at present the first two are not likely to cause too much concern. However, in both cases the level of risk to Mary could increase significantly if anything about the situation or Mary's behaviour were to change. These risks therefore need reviewing regularly, even though no action is currently needed. The second two areas of risk are of more concern. Risk (c) is perhaps the most worrying because there are a number of areas where the risk to Mary could be considerable. When we consider this risk in relation to the factors discussed above, the picture becomes clearer.

Detailed examination of the risk of sexual victimization for Mary

Frequency

Mary is visiting the shops very frequently, so the risk is present on a regular, and at least daily, basis.

LEVEL OF RISK

The likelihood of being sexually victimized is probably not great, given the kind of area in which Mary's home and the local shops are located. However, Mary's behaviour, and her readiness to become friendly and flirtatious, may be increasing the level of risk for her personally.

POSSIBLE OUTCOMES

The outcome of Mary being sexually victimized is potentially serious. She may be traumatized by the experience, may contract a sexually transmitted disease, may become pregnant, or might even, in the worst case, be murdered. Her family or carers would undoubtedly be very distressed, and staff may be held accountable. Mary may have to face the difficulties of parenthood, abortion, or even having a child that might be taken into care. It is possible that she might even suffer such distress as a result of the attack and its consequences that she becomes mentally ill, or even suicidal.

From the analysis above, it becomes clear that this is potentially a serious risk, and one that should be given attention, even though the likelihood of its occurrence is probably low. A number of strategies could be considered.

Management of the risk of victimization

1   *Mary is stopped from visiting the shops*
   Advantages. The risk to Mary is removed
   Disadvantages. Mary loses her freedom and sense of independence, together with a chance to integrate herself into her local community, where she is known.

2   *Mary continues going to the shops, but must be accompanied by a member of staff*
   Advantages. Mary is kept safe by her companion, but can still enjoy her shopping visits.
   Disadvantages. Mary loses her independence, and this activity 'ties up' a member of staff for the time that the shopping trip continues.

3 *Mary is taught to change her behaviour towards men, so that she becomes more reserved and wary of those she does not know*
Advantages. Mary retains her independence, and learns behaviour that is more socially acceptable.
Disadvantages. Mary may become fearful of strangers and uneasy about going out alone. It may also be difficult for her to learn new skills.

The risk-assessment meeting should discuss all possible options before deciding on a risk strategy. The difficulties here are that individual staff may favour particular approaches because of their own needs and attitudes. For example, care worker Maureen has herself been a victim of a sexual assault in the past. As a consequence she overestimates the level of risk to Mary, and feels strongly that Mary should only go out accompanied by a member of staff, preferably male. Care worker Joan, on the other hand, sees her role as being protective and motherly, and feels that the only sure way to keep Mary safe is to stop her going out. She dislikes the idea that a member of staff will be 'tied up' by going out with Mary, which she sees as 'pandering to' Mary. These kinds of responses need tactful handling by the home manager, who needs to set clear aims for the staff, perhaps related to the staff's role in promoting client independence and normalization.

In reality, what often decides the client's fate is not related to risk or choice as such, but to money and resources. Shortage of staff and poor client to staff ratios limit what staff can do with and for clients. It should be made clear in all risk assessments where the decision has been influenced by such considerations, rather than by considerations of the client's best interests.

The needs of the client also need to be balanced against the need of members of staff to feel secure. Refusing to allow Mary to go out, or insisting that she is accompanied, may seem to be the easiest solutions to the problem from the staff point of view, but they do not allow Mary any individual freedom or potential for growth. Teaching her to behave more appropriately and understand the potential risks for herself do both of these things. If people with learning disabilities are to genuinely be helped to live 'an ordinary life' then restricting her choices is not the solution.

Where staff carers or family members appear to be unreasonably restrictive in their attitudes, it may be worth confronting the problem by asking the following set of questions (see Lawson in Kemshall and Pritchard 1996):

- What does this person want in terms of outcome?
- Why do they want this?
- What do they value most?
- What anxieties do they have?

This may enable the other members of the group to explore how the needs and anxieties of this person can be met without limiting the opportunities of the person with learning disabilities. Wherever possible, *a solution which promotes the personal development of the person with learning disabilities should be the first choice*, unless this is likely to put others at risk.

It may be, however, that after a period of trying to teach Mary more appropriate behaviours, there is no sign of any change. If this is the case, then another strategy will have to be considered. For example, a member of staff could observe Mary from a safe distance, as she makes her shopping trips. Or it may be possible for her to be accompanied by another client, who is more circumspect about talking to strangers, and who will encourage Mary into more appropriate behaviours. Wherever possible the aim should be to help Mary increase her independence and variety of experiences, not reduce them.

Detailed assessment of the health risks for Mary

Risk (d) above, relating to buying excessive amounts of sweets and biscuits, is perhaps less serious, but also needs addressing:

Risk to Mary

This risk is also one that occurs frequently, in that Mary is visiting the shops every day, and sometimes more than once a day. Thus although buying sweets and biscuits is not a problem in itself, the frequency with which Mary is doing this is already affecting her weight, and her teeth, and may ultimately have more serious effects on her health.

Risks to others

There are no risks to others.

FREQUENCY

Mary is going to the shops and buying sweet things every day at least.

LEVEL OF RISK

The level of immediate risk is low. At this time, what Mary is doing appears relatively harmless.

POSSIBLE OUTCOMES

Mary is already gaining weight and having more fillings than she used to do. The longer-term risks have more serious potential outcomes. Mary may lose all her teeth and need false ones. She could develop diabetes or heart disease. The likelihood of these longer-term outcomes is uncertain, but they are increasingly likely to occur the more Mary consumes excessive amounts of sweet food and if she continues to gain weight.

Management of the health risks

It is clear from the above analysis that the problem lies not in what Mary is choosing to do, so much as in the frequency of her doing it. Many of us are in this situation: we eat, drink or smoke more than we should ideally do for the good of our health. At what point should we choose to intervene in Mary's choices?

To some extent this will be an arbitrary decision, but if as carers we have a duty of care to Mary, then perhaps we should begin to intervene at the point that her choices begin to have a measurably destructive effect, for example, if she is gaining weight to the point where she is clinically obese, or if she is having fillings every time she attends the dentist.

Strategies for managing this risk might be:

1 *Mary is stopped from visiting the shops*
   Advantages. Mary no longer obtains as many sweet things as previously and may therefore lose weight again, and have fewer fillings.
   Disadvantages. Mary loses her independence and freedom again.

She may also seek sweets and biscuits from elsewhere, such as from other residents.

2 *Mary's visits to the shops are limited*
Advantages. Mary still gets her shopping opportunities, but reducing them ensures she has fewer chances to buy sweets and biscuits.
Disadvantages. Mary will need to be much more closely monitored to ensure she does not leave the home several times. This may result in the door having to be locked, which would impact on other residents too. In addition, Mary will probably realize that her trips are being restricted, and may buy more on each trip as a consequence.

3 *Mary's money is controlled, so she cannot buy so much*
Advantages. Mary still has the freedom to go out and visit the shops, but her access to sweet things is restricted.
Disadvantages. This could limit Mary's ability to develop better understanding of the value of money, and how to budget for herself.

4 *Mary is given some health education about the likely implications of what she is doing, and the need to limit her intake of sweets and biscuits*
Advantages. This approach enables Mary to retain her independence and make choices for herself. However, it also means that she may choose not to change her habits.
Disadvantages. Mary may find it difficult to understand the risks she faces, and her choices may not coincide with what others feel is safe or appropriate.

In both these areas of risk, a balance has to be struck between the need to intervene to protect Mary, and the desire to enable her to have as much freedom as possible, including the freedom to make choices. The difficult issue for staff is to decide when they have to intervene. Ultimately this is often a personal decision, and is coloured by the needs and attitudes of the staff involved, as well as the availability of resources. By using a framework for decision-making, and involving as many people as possible (who know the client well), the process can be made less subjective and more explicit.

Finally, and most importantly, all the decisions made in the risk-assessment meeting *must* be documented and shared with all who are involved in Mary's care. This not only covers staff legally in that they can clearly demonstrate that any risk-taking had been fully discussed and agreed, but also helps to ensure that all involved in Mary's care are aware of the agreed strategies for managing risk, and are consistent in their approach to her.

However, it is equally important that this is not seen as a one-off exercise. Risks change all the time, and Mary herself will also change and develop, especially if the skills teaching is successful. Regular reviews of risks and agreed strategies for their management are vital. There is absolutely no point in undertaking a skills-teaching programme if Mary is not allowed to make use of what she has learned.

Summary

Although the aim for those working with people with learning disabilities should be to promote choice and independence as far as possible, there will always be some people who have difficulty in making choices without help. In addition to their learning disabilities, some will suffer from problems related to their early life, and some will have problems such as mental illness or epilepsy, which may make life more difficult and risky for them. These clients will need additional support and help to deal with everyday life. Such conditions make the assessment of risk more difficult for them, and others may need to take on that responsibility for them.

Choice and risk are part of everyday life for most of us. We assess risks for ourselves all the time, even though we probably do not do it particularly well. However, when we have to do it for someone else it becomes much more difficult, and ethically questionable, because any negative outcome affects the other person, not us directly. The approach suggested in this chapter is not infallible, but it aims to give a structure within which everyday risks can be evaluated and discussed. What is interesting, when the alternatives are examined closely, is that the easiest options are not necessarily the best options for the client. The best options will include the need to actively help the client to learn and grow, so that there is the chance to learn how to make better choices and decisions unaided. This requires concerted and organized effort on the part of those who work with clients, and even then there is no guarantee that they will be able to learn everything necessary to make the 'best' (i.e. safest) choices. However, if our role is truly to assist clients in their personal development in every way, then trying to teach them to make better choices and assess risk more effectively is the option that we should be taking. Only if that approach fails, and we are seriously worried about their health or safety, should alternatives be sought.

A structured approach to the assessment and management of risk will include consideration of the factors which relate to that particular person, their level of ability, their problems and their abilities. It will also consider the environmental factors, including how often risks are taken, the level of risk in terms of the likelihood of it occurring, and the possible outcomes, both good and bad. Only after consideration of all these factors can a realistic strategy for managing risk be drawn up. It is worth noting, however, that it is rarely possible to eliminate risk. Life is risky, and risk assessors need to accept that sometimes things will go wrong. Good management strategies will include some attempt to minimize harm, if the worst happens.

chapter four

EVERYDAY RISKS

Risks at Home

Much of the previous work on risk assessment has focused on the risks associated with violent crime. Less has been done on the risks associated with everyday living, not because they are necessarily less significant, but perhaps because we are all so used to living with them. Let us consider for a moment some of the risks that are present during the course of a relatively ordinary day.

A typical day

Even being in bed is dangerous. More people die in bed than anywhere else! Getting out of bed is fraught with danger. People have been known to strain their back turning over in bed. Getting out of bed could lead to a fall. A worn carpet or slippery floor in the bedroom or bathroom could also lead to a fall. If a person is poorly co-ordinated, tired, over-medicated, elderly, blind, or otherwise physically impaired, this may increase the risk to them of one of these events occurring.

Eating may lead to choking, as may drinking. Some food or drink could cause vomiting, or could even lead to an allergic reaction, which can be life-threatening. Overeating on a consistent basis might lead to bad teeth or obesity. Drinking too much coffee can produce unpleasant symptoms of agitation, or gastric problems. In some people excessive caffeine can produce behavioural problems such as overactivity. An excessively hot drink could cause scalding and burns.

Washing, bathing, or washing up could all be dangerous because the water used may be too hot, and scalding could result. Some people may be poorly co-ordinated, so that they are more likely to break things. They may then cut themselves on fragments of china or glass. Splashed water could again put someone at risk of a fall. Making the beds could result in a back injury from awkward bending or lifting. Using the vacuum cleaner may result in muscle strain, electric shock, or even electrocution. Dusting could lead to an asthma attack and possible death. Going shopping could result in a fall, a robbery, or a road accident.

It can be seen from all of the above that there are indeed risks in almost everything we do. However, the reason that most of us cope with these risks without thinking about them most of the time is that we take steps, as far as we can, to ensure that the level of risk is relatively low. What is important here is to identify the various factors which contribute to risk, and look at how these may be managed or reduced. More accidents occur in the home than anywhere else, but because our own home is so familiar to us we tend to ignore or minimize these risks most of the time.

Risk factors can be broken down into those which relate to the environment and those which relate to the individual. It may be helpful to examine these separately.

FACTORS RELATING TO THE ENVIRONMENT

It can be seen from the above outlines that many aspects of the environment can contribute to risk. Carpets and other flooring materials should be regularly inspected and maintained, and electrical items should be regularly serviced. Furnishings and appliances should be suitable and not easily damaged. This kind of maintenance is largely covered by the legal requirements of the Health and Safety Act, but sometimes risks are overlooked simply because they are commonplace, and everyone has got used to seeing them.

Other environmental factors will include such things as the levels of staffing available, and the nature of the other clients in the home. Clients who are inclined to assault others obviously increase the levels of risk for other clients and staff alike, and appropriate strategies to manage their behaviour are vital to keep other residents and staff as safe as possible. Here, careful supervision is often the key to avoiding risk, as is good management of the environment, but once again it is probably impossible to eliminate risk.

FACTORS RELATING TO THE INDIVIDUAL

Each person will bring different abilities and problems to the situation. As discussed in the previous chapter, there are a number of individual characteristics which will tend to increase the likelihood of someone taking risks unnecessarily, being a risk to others, or failing to perceive or understand the risks they are taking. While some of these, such as some forms of mental illness, may be amenable to change, many of them, such as the effects of brain injury, or dementia, will probably not be. In some cases, it may be possible to change the risks associated with a given individual by means of specific education. Where possible, the aim should be to reduce risks that are related to the individual in ways that do not restrict that person's freedom and choice.

Frequency and likelihood of risks occurring

The likelihood of any given event occurring is also variable, and some negative outcomes are distinctly less likely than others. Managing risk requires that people attempt to make some assessment of how likely each outcome is, and act accordingly. For example, although many people die in bed, we recognize that the reasons for this happening are usually related to age, or particular situations or illnesses, and although statistically this is a risk, it is not one that seems very significant to most of us when we climb into bed each night.

Similarly, although eating and drinking may lead to choking, for most of us this risk is not very great. Some individuals may have specific problems in eating or swallowing, however, which may make this a much greater risk for them. Knowledge of the individual is essential in managing this type of risk. However, it is also important to try and obtain some realistic assessment of the true statistical probability of any given risk occurring. There is often a tendency to overestimate risk for others and underestimate it for ourselves.

Interaction of risk factors

In most cases, the level of risk in any given situation is the result of an interaction of factors. Thus environmental, personal and statistical factors are all relevant in the assessment of risk. An elderly, frail person in a poorly maintained home, where there are frequent changes of staff, is at much greater risk of accidental injury than the same person would be in a well-maintained home where staff know him or her well. In the latter situation, the environmental risks have been minimized, and the staff's knowledge of that person and their particular problems and difficulties will help them to ensure that he or she is kept as safe as possible. If someone is physically frail or disabled, it may be necessary to provide one-to-one assistance in order to ensure safety. Similarly, if a client is impulsive and unable to understand the nature of risk for themselves then close supervision may be the only way to reduce risk for them, without severely curtailing their life experiences. Unfortunately, good supervision tends to be expensive in terms of staff time, and too often the decision is to limit freedom rather than provide the necessary level of care and supervision. Where care provision is driven by budgets rather than actual need, the level of care and personal freedom is always going to be limited by cost.

Planning services to minimize risk

Risks in the home therefore need to be managed, just as risks outside the home would be. Home managers need to make sure that the physical environment is as safe as possible, and that staffing levels allow the appropriate level of supervision and care to be given. This may not just mean that there need to be enough staff to watch over clients. As will be described later in this book, effective risk management will sometimes involve considerable input from skilled staff. Unfortunately such issues are not always easily resolved, and, as noted above, cost factors often hold sway over clinical and safety concerns. In these situations, home managers have a duty to try and obtain the minimum standard which they feel is necessary, and to take these issues to a higher authority if their concerns are not taken seriously by their managers.

Assessing Skills

A large part of avoiding everyday risks is having the skills to cope with everyday events. An awareness of the kinds of risks posed by electrical equipment, for example, can enable someone to treat such equipment with extra care, thereby avoiding danger. People with learning disabilities often have limited opportunities to acquire skills that most of us take for granted. Taking the time to teach them about the risks posed by activities in everyday life can help to reduce their vulnerability and reassure those who care from them that they can safely be allowed more independence.

Within the home, people need to understand how the various appliances work, and what to do if something goes wrong. It is relatively straightforward to observe how well someone can operate a piece of domestic equipment, and to assess whether they could safely use it alone. People can often be taught how to use fire-blankets, or change a fuse. The difficult part is teaching them to have to capacity to judge when such things should be done. Many relatively able people with learning disabilities lack judgement, and it is this feature rather than any other which often renders them vulnerable.

The capacity to assess risk for oneself requires that one has the ability to envisage the outcome of any given course of action. It is this ability to foresee the consequences of one's actions or choices which is crucial to safety. It is related to the ability to use feedback and to plan and organize one's actions accordingly. It is the lack of this ability which makes many otherwise reasonably able people vulnerable. One can try to assess these abilities in people with learning disabilities by asking them questions about hypothetical situations. For example, 'What could happen if you left the cooker on all night?' or 'Why shouldn't you talk to strangers?'

Of course this approach relies on the person having sufficient language to be able to understand the questions and give an account of their likely responses. However, even when the client's speech and language are good, it may be that they can give an acceptable account of what they *should* do, but in fact will not do it when the situation actually occurs. This is not necessarily a wilful intent to deceive but more often a problem with one particular area of memory. When they are faced with a given situation they respond immediately and automatically, without recalling the information they have learned previously.

Over time, it is usually possible to build up a picture of how any given individual will respond in any situation. This requires that staff spend time getting to know the person, and observing them in a number of different situations. Thus in order to be able to assess risk meaningfully, *there is no substitute for knowing your client well.* Of course this can be a problem when the home manager is faced with high turnover of staff, many of whom will be relatively young and inexperienced. Their knowledge of people with learning disabilities generally will probably be limited, and their knowledge of the clients in this particular home equally so. Consequently it is vital not only to record in written form any risk assessments that are completed, but also to ensure that care staff and others responsible for the client's safety *actually read them, and understand their implications.* This should be an important part of their induction, and should not be left to chance. It is essential to the effective management of risk in the home.

One recurring difficulty is that staff are inclined to make unwarranted assumptions about a client's abilities and motivations. Typically carers attribute wilfulness or stubbornness where often there is simply only forgetfulness or fear. It is very important to try and ensure that staff have a realistic understanding of their clients' problems. Training is vital here, as is having relevant books available in the home. If there is doubt about a client's level of understanding, then a psychological assessment and/or a speech therapy assessment can be invaluable. Very often clients are misrepresented and misunderstood. They may be treated punitively because staff assume wilful non-compliance, when actually clients simply cannot remember what they have been told, or are unable to put existing skills into practice.

Going Out: Alone or with Others

As more and more people with learning disabilities have moved into the community, the issue of whether they should be allowed out alone has become more and more significant. In reality the average community home tends to have the front door locked, and residents are only allowed to leave when accompanied by staff. In many cases this may be because it seems to be the only realistic way to keep the residents safe. They may have very limited language, or be impulsive, or they may have no road sense.

It is easy to both overestimate and underestimate the range of risks that we all face on an everyday basis. As described at the beginning of this chapter, most everyday activities carry a risk. The reason we are not all paralysed with fear is that we know these risks are relatively small, that is, they are not very likely to occur. Where we can, we take steps to minimize those risks. Also we are often happy to take risks for ourselves, but much less happy to allow those in our care to take the same risks. Enabling people with learning disabilities to take the same risks as the rest of us may be important in allowing them to develop the 'normal life' that should be the goal of community homes.

For those clients who do go out unaccompanied there are often real concerns. They may behave inappropriately, and cause concern amongst the rest of the community. They may behave in ways which put them at risk of abuse or assault. Sometimes these difficulties remain resistant to change, but on many occasions there is an issue about skills teaching. Staff who care for these clients may sometimes take the easy option, and lock the door or always accompany people, rather than take the time and trouble to teach a resident how to do something alone. Indeed this can apply both inside and outside the home. If the goal of services for people with learning disabilities is truly to improve their quality of life, and enable them to lead a 'normal life' then it would seem more important to help clients develop their own skills rather than continue their dependence on others.

For example, some time spent teaching someone how to deal with money may reduce the risk of financial exploitation by others. Teaching someone how to cross the road safely may reduce the risk of injury, and also the need for staff to accompany them each time they go out. Taking time to try and teach new skills may actually lighten the burden on care staff. It also changes the nature of their job from a focus on carrying out practical tasks for the clients to one of enabling the clients to grow and develop.

However, if this is to happen, then this responsibility has to be made explicit, and acknowledged as valuable. The role of care staff needs to be much more highly valued than it has been. Without them, people with learning disabilities will find it much harder to make progress. Currently care staff are often among the least trained, least valued and worst paid workers in society, yet they are increasingly expected to do a complex and demanding job, which carries considerable responsibility for other people's lives.

Problems with Skills Teaching

One of the recurring problems with skills teaching is that it is time-consuming. When staff are under pressure, or staffing levels are lower than they should be, it is often seen as easier to do a task oneself, or to prevent the client taking a risk, than to take the time to teach them the necessary skills. Also, as discussed previously, even after concerted attempts at skills teaching there will be ongoing difficulties with some clients. In spite of repeated attempts to modify their more worrying behaviour, and teach them appropriate skills, some people with learning disabilities remain unable to implement those skills effectively. In these cases it is imperative that supervision by staff continues. The important point here is that the attempt has been made, consistently and carefully, to allow that individual to extend their skills repertoire, *before* assuming that they are unable to do something. It may also be that repeated attempts will eventually bear fruit. Remember that clients have a *learning disability*, i.e. they need longer to learn than most people do.

Another problem with skills teaching, however, is that most of our social interactions are extremely complex. Often the need is not just to develop a single skill, but rather to develop a repertoire of related skills, and to know which to use when. For example, it is relatively easy to teach someone the skill of politely greeting others with a 'Good morning'. Teaching them when and how it is appropriate to say it is more difficult. Again we return to the problem of a lack of judgement. Very often this is the characteristic which renders people with learning disabilities most vulnerable. It becomes a very significant problem when the individual is relatively able, and wishes to engage in something closer to the 'normal life' that they see everyone else having.

FRED

Fred enjoys a pint of beer, like many men. His favourite occupation is going out with friends and having a drink. Unfortunately, Fred is not very good at 'holding his drink' and will easily get quite drunk. After three or four pints he can become aggressive and soon after this will often vomit. In addition, Fred does not have much money, and he often spends a large part of his spare money on drinks for himself and those around him. Staff feel that other people exploit Fred's generosity, but Fred insists that he wants to spend his money in this way. Despite many attempts at counselling him, this pattern of behaviour persists. As a result, staff are reluctant to take Fred out for a drink because they often have problems managing his behaviour afterwards. Neither do they feel confident to let Fred go out drinking unaccompanied.

Assessment of risks

RISKS TO FRED

Fred knows that many men go out for drinks with their friends, and some get drunk. His father used to do the same, and Fred wants to do what other men do. He resents being treated 'like a child' as he sees it. However, staff who accompany him are concerned that he is being exploited by other people who see him as a 'soft touch' for a drink, and they are also worried about how ill he becomes if he drinks too much. On one occasion he ended up in hospital because he could not stop vomiting. They are also worried that his aggressive behaviour when drunk could result in him getting into a fight.

The risks here centre around the effects on Fred's health and personal safety, and the way in which he spends all his money on drink. While he will tell staff that it is his money to use as he pleases, there are also often problems in the home subsequently, because when Fred has no money for cigarettes he pesters other residents to give him money or cigarettes. This leads to stresses and conflicts in the home. Repeated attempts to help Fred understand the risks he is taking have met with limited success. While he appears to understand what he is being told, and will even agree to some extent, he persists in repeating the same pattern.

Several staff in the home feel that Fred is just stubborn and difficult. They consider that Fred is out to rebel and 'wind them up'. However, the true picture is slightly different. Fred has a very poor short-term memory, especially for verbal material. Thus although he can understand the arguments put to him when he is at home and sober, once he is out having a good time he forgets what has been said to him. Furthermore, as anyone who drinks knows, alcohol is very good at suppressing one's better intentions, and it is easy to go out, 'just for one' and come home having had far too many. Fred is just as much at risk of this as anyone else.

In order to manage Fred's behaviour, it is important to understand the nature of his difficulties and deal with the situation accordingly. Attributing 'stubbornness' or 'wilfulness' to him does not help the situation, and simply traps the staff into feeling frustrated and angry with Fred.

RISKS TO OTHERS

Fred may become aggressive and even violent if confronted when drunk.

FREQUENCY

If Fred is drinking every night, then there is real cause for concern. Drinking heavily every night will not only use all his money, but also put him at real risk of damaging his health, especially if he is getting seriously drunk every night. If, however, it is once a month, then the level of concern and risk is much less. It is also important to assess how often Fred drinks and becomes ill, or aggressive, against how often he drinks but is just a bit 'merry'. So far, however, it would seem that there are several risks which are encountered quite frequently.

LEVEL OF RISK

How likely is it that Fred will do real damage to his health? What are the statistics associated with drinking and related health problems? It is generally accepted now that drinking every night is probably not desirable, but that moderate drinking, of say two pints of beer, on three or four nights a week, will probably do no harm. His aggressiveness seems to be directly related to the amount he is drinking, so reducing the frequency and quantity of his drinking will presumably also reduce the risk of his getting into a fight. If he did get into a fight he is not likely to be able to defend himself effectively and is at real risk of physical harm.

Similarly, if Fred is spending a lot of money on others every night, his money will soon be gone. In addition, the consequent lack of money leads to a real risk of conflict in the home, when he nags others to give him money or cigarettes to replace his own. However, if Fred goes out and spends his money on one evening a month, then there is less chance that he will spend all his money. Thus the level of risk here seems to depend on how often Fred is drinking, and how much.

POSSIBLE OUTCOMES

In the short term the negative outcomes are that Fred vomits, uses all his money and may become aggressive. He puts himself and others at risk of getting into a fight. In the longer term, he may damage his brain, liver and general health by excessive drinking, and if he uses all his money other problems within the home may escalate, eventually resulting in him having to leave the home and move elsewhere.

Management of risks

None of the outcomes described above could be considered to be in Fred's interests. However, he does enjoy a drink, and the social contact that this brings. He likes to feel that he is 'one of the boys'. Fred assesses the short-term benefits of his drinking and feels that he wishes to continue. He does not appear to really understand the long-term implications of his behaviour, and his memory problems make it particularly difficult for him to remember them when he is out drinking. Of course, many people who do not have a learning disability, or memory problems, will similarly lose sight of their good intentions once they have had a drink or two.

For staff who have a duty of care to Fred, it seems clear that some compromise needs to be reached. Fred expresses a choice to go out and drink with friends, and it would seem appropriate to let him make that choice. The difficulty lies in the possible negative outcomes that follow from this choice.

Since the level of risk seems to be directly related to the frequency of Fred's drinking, then the logical approach here would seem to be to limit the number of occasions on which Fred is allowed to go drinking. In addition it would be beneficial to limit both how much he drinks on any one occasion, as well as how much money he takes with him. Of course, limiting his money will also limit his drinking to some extent.

Obtaining Fred's co-operation may be difficult, but it may be possible to establish some kind of contract with him. For example, that going out drinking is conditional upon an agreement that he will only drink two pints at any one sitting, and will take no more than a certain sum of money. If this kind of contract cannot be established, then it may be necessary to ensure that Fred is accompanied whenever he goes drinking, to remind him of the possible outcomes.

This scenario illustrates clearly the dilemma that many care staff face. On the one hand they are encouraged to offer their clients choice, but on the other they are told that they must manage the risks that the clients face, and take responsibility for their safety. Although it is no longer acceptable to consider people with learning disabilities as overgrown children, a comparison with how children are given choice and freedom may help to clarify one's thinking. As discussed before, as children grow up, it is usual to extend the degree of choice and freedom that they are given, according to their level of understanding and skill. When children are very young, and their appreciation of risk is limited, parents tend to be protective, and to keep them under supervision much of the time. As they get older and more able to judge risks for themselves, then parents will usually allow them more freedom and opportunities to make choices and take risks. To some extent, parents usually allow children to make their own mistakes and learn from them, assuming that the consequences of the choices are not too serious.

As discussed previously, people with learning disabilities have often had very limited opportunities to learn from their own mistakes, and they tend to learn more slowly anyway. Thus sometimes it can be helpful to enable them to make mistakes in the same way that growing children do. However, often the person with learning disabilities does not appear to learn from experience in the same way as a person without learning disabilities would do, or they may take much longer to learn. In these situations, it may be necessary for care staff to limit their choices in order to keep them safe from harm or exploitation.

Clients like Fred are commonplace, and it is a skilled job to draw the line between allowing personal choice, freedom and opportunities for development, and keeping the person safe from harm. Where care staff feel unable or reluctant to make such decisions, it may be helpful to seek advice from others involved in that person's care. However, in reality the buck will often stop with the care staff, who are faced with making often difficult decisions at a crucial moment. It is important that the staff team work together to agree a consistent approach to managing risks for clients like Fred, and that the decisions about risk-taking are agreed with managers, and well documented. This protects both the client and the staff. Generally, if it can be demonstrated that any decisions were carefully considered and were made in what was believed to be the client's best interests, then the law will accept that as valid.

In Sickness and in Health: Medical Risks

The management of risk in relation to health care can be particularly difficult. Decisions about health care require an understanding of both the short- and long-term implications of the choice made. How far should someone be allowed to ignore their health care? What are the implications of not cleaning one's teeth regularly? Should a diabetic who loves biscuits and chocolate be allowed to choose how much she or he eats? If a serious operation is required, who decides whether it should take place?

The issue of assessing risk in these situations is closely allied to the issue of informed consent. In order to choose a given course of action, the person concerned must understand what the implications of that choice will be. Understanding implies that they can remember and repeat what they have been told, even after a delay of several days. It also implies that they can truly appreciate what the possible outcome will mean. It also implies some idea of alternatives.

In the examples above, 'the choice' to not clean one's teeth, may result from lack of understanding about what can happen if teeth are neglected, or it may simply reflect a lack of skill. Even if, however, the skill is there but not used, it may be that nobody has taken time to explain why teeth should be cleaned, or what may happen if they are not. It may be a memory problem (the client simply forgets to clean their teeth), or it could be a motivational one (the client simply cannot get around to doing it without prompting). The consequences here can be both medical and social (bad teeth and/or social rejection).

Where the client's 'choice' not to clean their teeth is the result of ignorance about the consequences, it cannot be seen as a real choice. In these circumstances, if there is evidence that the person has a difficulty in understanding the consequences, then there is a duty of care for the care staff. They need to ensure that teeth are cleaned to a degree that ensures that health is not adversely affected.

The same argument applies to the diabetic who wishes to eat lots of biscuits and chocolate. While a small amount, carefully monitored, may be allowable, excessive amounts of these sugary foods can be truly dangerous to a diabetic, both in terms of short- and long-term consequences. In this situation, where there is any doubt about the understanding of the person concerned, care staff must take responsibility for the control of such foods. Nevertheless, there should still be attempts made over time to educate the person about their condition, in which case they may eventually be able to take at least some responsibility for their own care. A major difficulty with this kind of choice is that the short-term gains (eating sweet things) will tend to override the consideration of long-term consequences (the health risks). This is a problem faced by everyone, not just people with learning disabilities.

The process of education

Health education can be difficult because long-term effects on health are slow to show themselves, and often difficult to imagine. The short-term pleasures which come from substances such as sweets, biscuits, alcohol or nicotine, in contrast, are immediate. In addition, people cannot see their internal organs, or how they work. Knowledge of hospitals and operations may only have been acquired via television. Symptoms may occur, but not be recognized as being significant. For example, it is particularly difficult to communicate concepts such as 'pain' to someone with very little language. Pictures and picture sequences, as well as short films, can often be helpful in communicating basic information to clients. For those who are familiar with signs, signing can be used. However, with people with severe learning disabilities even these aids may not be particularly helpful. In these cases care staff must take responsibility for health care, and observe their clients closely. Where risks are taken, these must be agreed to be acceptable by everyone involved in the care of that person.

Whose responsibility?

When it is clear that people are unable to make a real choice about a health issue, for example in deciding whether to have an operation, then a decision has to be made about who will make the choice for them. In earlier times, such choices were often made by parents (even of adult children), or by the medical consultant responsible for the person's care. More recently, the law has changed, and now only the professional responsible for the intervention can make the final decision. Thus if the person cannot make the choice for themselves, the doctor or surgeon concerned must decide if the action is reasonable. Some doctors still resist this responsibility. This is not surprising, because if they are deemed to be in error they run the risk of being accused of assault.

Even where the surgeon or doctor is willing to make the decision whether to treat or not, he or she will often seek information from those who know the client well. This usually means family or care staff. In these situations the risk can be assessed, as before, using the dimensions already outlined – nature of risk, frequency, level and outcome (both short- and long-term) – but with additional information from medical sources.

ROSIE

Rosie has a problem with her wisdom teeth. The dentist has told her keyworker that she will need to have two of them removed. She has a recurring abscess under one of them, and the other is impacted. Rosie is terrified of the dentist anyway, and her keyworker is worried that if she has to have her wisdom teeth out, he will never be able to get her to the dentist again.

Assessment of risks

RISKS TO ROSIE

Rosie is at risk from the physical effects of the abscess under her tooth. Even if the infection is treated, it could recur. At worst this could lead to septicaemia. She is also at risk of recurring toothache. However, there is also a risk that, if handled badly, her treatment could result in her becoming fearful of the dentist, which could also have longer-term implications for her health. There is a small risk that she could die under the anaesthetic.

RISK TO OTHERS

There is no risk to others.

FREQUENCY

Rosie, like everyone else, only has four wisdom teeth, so there is a low risk that she will need this operation more than once. If she does not have the operation, there is a risk of repeated infection in the tooth with the abscess, and from pain from the impacted tooth. These events could recur quite often. However, if she develops an increased fear of going to the dentist, this could cause significant long-term problems in managing her dental health, as she usually attends every six months for a check-up. If Rosie became negative about the dentist this may therefore make it difficult to maintain her dental health in the future.

LEVEL OF RISK

There is a risk that Rosie could die under a general anaesthetic, but this is low. There is also a moderate risk of an infection developing post-operatively, although this would probably be relatively easily treated. Chronic post-operative infection is also possible, but is still relatively rare. However, if she were to have her wisdom teeth removed under local anaesthetic, there is a risk that she may become fearful of the dentist. If she does *not* have the operation, there is a fairly high likelihood that she will continue to have pain from her teeth, and a slightly lower level of risk that her overall health will be affected in time.

POSSIBLE OUTCOMES (SHORT- AND LONG-TERM)

In the short term Rosie is likely to suffer pain and anxiety. However, in the slightly longer term she should suffer fewer problems and less pain from her teeth if she has the operation. If her wisdom teeth are not removed she is likely to suffer recurrent pain and infection, and there is always a possibility of more serious infection developing. On balance, although there are risks associated with the operation, these are largely one-off risks, while the risks associated with not carrying out the operation are recurrent.

Management of risks

From this analysis, it would seem clear that the best course of action would probably be to remove the troublesome wisdom teeth, but to spend some time preparing Rosie for the experience. She could visit the dentist's surgery to see how the anaesthetic is given, with an explanation of how she will be asleep and therefore unable to feel anything. However, it is also important to explain to Rosie that there will be some pain and discomfort afterwards, but that will soon go, and that the operation should reduce her problems with her teeth in the long term. Whether or not the choice should be Rosie's or the surgeon's will depend on how well Rosie is able to understand the different possible outcomes, and how serious the dental surgeon thinks the problem may be. Rosie's capacity to consent should be independently assessed.

In assessing the risks associated with serious medical interventions it is always important to obtain information from qualified medical staff. In terms of more general health care, it may be necessary to ensure that the person with a learning disability has received basic health-care information in a form which they can understand. In both situations, it may be necessary to take the choice out of the hands of the person with a learning disability, if it appears that they are genuinely unable to understand the risks they are taking.

Having said that, it should be borne in mind that we all take risks with our health, and people with learning disabilities should be allowed to take some of those risks if they choose, as long as they do have some understanding of the likely implications. For example, most of us in Western society eat too much, are slightly overweight and do not take enough exercise. A lot of us smoke and drink too much alcohol. It seems unreasonable to insist that people with learning disabilities should be any different from the rest of us.

Relationships and Consent

This is perhaps one of the most difficult areas in terms of both risk assessment and consent. The choice to engage in a relationship, particularly a sexual one, opens up a whole range of potential risks which are not easy to manage. These were discussed at some length in chapter 1. Engaging in sexual relationships means that one runs the risk of abuse, exploitation, sexually transmitted disease (including HIV), pregnancy (with all its associated risks) and parenthood.

Educating people with learning disabilities about all these possible risks is a huge task, but one which, ethically, should be undertaken if they are to engage in sexual relationships. Thus one of the first responsibilities of care staff who may become aware that one of their clients may be involved in a sexual relationship should be to refer them to a clinical psychologist for sex education, or to undertake it themselves. In addition, the psychologist should be asked for an opinion about their capacity to consent to a sexual relationship. Unless there is clear evidence that the person is able to consent in a real sense (that is with a full understanding of what the likely consequences may be), then care staff *have a duty to ensure that the person does not engage in sexual activities with others.* If they do not do so, then care staff run the risk of being held responsible in law for any adverse consequences.

One of the difficulties with this position is that, if one examines the behaviour of most adults in society, it is questionable how many of them consider all the potential risks associated with engaging in a sexual relationship. It is possible that we are insisting on a level of competence for people with learning disabilities which is greater than that required of the average man or woman. This seems a little unfair. Nevertheless, as the law stands, that is the position. Where vulnerable clients have been abused or exploited, the care staff may be held responsible in law for what has happened to them.

As the law currently stands, it is decreed that anyone who has a severe learning disability is not capable of giving informed consent to a sexual relationship. The definition of 'severe learning disability' is problematic. Frequently someone is assumed to have a 'severe learning disability' if their IQ falls below 55. However, this is by no means as clear-cut as it sounds. Psychologists know that people will produce different IQ scores on different occasions. Usually these differences are small (a few points), but they can be much greater. These variations could make the difference between apparently having a learning disability and being considered normal, or between having a significant learning disability and a severe learning disability. In practice, large changes are rare, but variations of several points or so either way are not. In addition, different IQ tests will give different results, with some tests always giving slightly higher results than others. This is why psychologists are often reluctant to quote actual figures for IQ, and it makes the implementation of a cut-off of 55 very difficult. At best such a figure can only be a guide, and other aspects of the person's abilities also need to be considered. In particular, it is important to assess, in addition, their level of language ability and comprehension, and their social and practical skills.

Where a sexual relationship is between carer and client, the law has always been clear. The carer has been said to be exploiting a position of trust, just as a doctor would be said to do, if a sexual relationship develops. However, a recent court case in the UK, when a judge decreed that a woman with severe learning disabilities was 'following her natural instincts' by submitting to sexual advances from one of her carers, has thrown this into question. It was argued that she did not resist his approaches, and sought him out. However, most carers would find this unacceptable and it seems likely that this judgement will be challenged.

It becomes even more difficult when two clients seek to have a sexual relationship and both of them have learning disabilities. Where one is more able than the other, there is a risk of exploitation occurring. Issues such as the physical strength of one partner against the other, and who initiates sexual contact (or indeed any contact) become important here. Where the initiator is always the same person, this should be a cause for concern. Coercion need not be physical, and threats or sulking can often be just as abusive psychologically as actual violence.

Where both clients have severe learning disabilities, the situation becomes even more difficult. Although one might argue that there is more equality in such situations, this does not ensure that there will be no coercion. In addition, the law states that if neither party has the cognitive capacity to understand what they are undertaking, as well as its likely consequences, the person or people should not be engaging in sexual relationships. While some may feel that this is unnecessarily harsh, from the legal point of view care staff are putting themselves at risk if they allow such relationships to develop or continue. Even where both clients have severe learning disabilities it is still possible that one party is being exploited. Where language is limited, it is often very difficult to be certain whether or not this is occurring. There is no question here that staff have a duty of care to keep both parties safe.

Sexual 'offending'

Where clients have a propensity for inappropriate sexual behaviour, care staff also have a difficult task. If clients approach other clients or members of staff in a sexually inappropriate way, technically it is a sexual offence. In practice, many clients and staff tolerate such approaches, and rarely would such behaviour come to the attention of the police. However, if such behaviour were directed towards an ordinary member of the public it is much more likely that they would perceive it as an offence, and this may lead to police intervention. In such situations, clients need to be protected from their own impulses, and others need to be protected from them.

It is important to make a distinction between those who are unaware of social rules and those who are aware but unconcerned. Some quite severely impaired individuals are still aware enough to target vulnerable victims (e.g. non-verbal fellow-clients in wheelchairs) and will limit their behaviour to places where they know they are less likely to be detected. These problems will be discussed more fully in a later chapter.

Summary

Everyday life is risky. We all take risks all the time. For most of us these are so familiar and frequent that we give them little thought. It is only when we are given responsibility for others' lives that assessing risk becomes a problem. The reality is, of course, that we assess risk for ourselves very poorly. Our decisions are biased by our wishes and desires for short-term gains, and are not wholly rational. In assessing risks for others we need to be more rational, and try to explicitly balance their needs and wishes against our feelings of responsibility. Consideration needs to be given to all the ways in which risks can be reduced, and wherever possible the aim should be to increase the client's capacity to assess and cope with risks for themselves. This may require skills teaching, as well as ongoing assessment of a person's capacity to make choices and judgements. Wherever possible, the client's freedom to make some choices should be maintained, even where the management of the risks means that some limits do have to be placed around their freedom. Sometimes a person's freedom will need to be limited to some degree to protect them, or to protect others from them. This should not be done lightly.

Careful analysis of each situation, using a structured approach, should enable the quality of decision-making about each client to be improved. While problems will not disappear, the process enables carers and professionals to feel more confident about the strategies they adopt, and where necessary allow them to justify their decisions to any higher authority.

chapter five

PARENTS WITH LEARNING DISABILITIES

If people with learning disabilities enter into sexual relationships then one possible outcome is that at some stage pregnancy and parenthood may result. Even if effective contraception is understood and used there will be the occasional failures, and some people with learning disabilities, like the rest of us, will actively want to become parents. This chapter attempts to look at the implications of parenthood for people with learning disabilities.

Choosing to be Parents versus Contraception, Abortion, or Sterilization

In earlier days, people with learning disabilities were denied the right to parenthood by strict segregation of the sexes, or compulsory sterilization. To some extent these practices continue, albeit in a less obviously draconian form. However, the Human Rights Act gives all human beings the right to marry and found a family, and thus it is likely that increasing numbers of people with learning disabilities may choose to become parents in future years.

The difficulty with this is that, although there may be a right to found a family, the care and upbringing of that family may require a level of skill and ability which is beyond that of the learning disabled parent. At one time the major objection to learning-disabled parents was the fear that they would increase the population of learning-disabled people to an impossible level by producing more and more handicapped babies. Evidence does not support this, and many parents with learning disabilities can and do have normal babies. However, concerns now tend to centre on the care of the child or children. Growing children present their parents with a great many challenges, practical, psychological and emotional. The concern is that a parent with learning disabilities may not have the ability or adaptability to deal with these challenges as they arise. In practice, sadly, many of the children of parents with learning disabilities end up in the care of social services.

One of the main areas of difficulty for parents with learning disabilities is that of judgement. Again and again in the discussion of risk assessment, this issue of judgement, or the lack of it, becomes the key. Parents need to be able to foresee danger and take action in advance to protect their children adequately. They need to be able to problem-solve in the here and now. Many parents with learning disabilities lack this capacity for judgement, and while they may manage a very young baby safely, once the child becomes more active and independent they are no longer able to keep it safe. Thus it is not that parents with learning disabilities are less loving, or more likely to abuse their children. It is, however, more likely that they are unable to keep them safe, either in the physical environment or from the risks presented by other people.

In considering risks associated with parenthood, therefore, there are not just the physical risks associated with pregnancy and birth to be examined, but also the very real risk that the child will be removed from the parents' care. There is a significant risk of exposure to a great deal of emotional stress and distress as a consequence of the latter.

Sex education, contraception and the risks of sexually transmitted diseases

Parenthood should ideally be a choice, not an accident. Thus any client who is believed to be sexually active, or interested in being so, should receive basic sex education. This should include education about types of contraception and how they work. It should also include information about sexually transmitted diseases and 'safe sex' in relation to HIV infection. While the incidence of such diseases is still relatively low in many countries, and one might argue that this is a low risk, it is still important that clients are aware of the risks they may run. As discussed earlier in the section on the general assessment of risk, while the likelihood of contracting disease may be low, for HIV in particular the ultimate outcome is very serious. Currently there is no effective cure, and the eventual outcome is death.

This kind of education is particularly important where there is a suspicion that clients are taking part in anal sex, which is known to carry higher risks of HIV infection. However, as with the rest of the population, some clients may know the risks but choose to ignore them. The important issue for care staff and professionals is that they have done their best to ensure that the information is given and understood. If they are not confident that this is the case, then for their own protection clients should be prevented from engaging in such activities. Many women with learning disabilities are given contraception by means of regular injections every three months or so. While this can protect them against unwanted pregnancy, it cannot protect them against sexually transmitted diseases. It is also important that clients should understand the reasons for such injections, and be aware of the risks they may involve. This is a form of medical treatment, and all the issues outlined previously apply here also. There is a duty of care, and medical staff who give such injections without informed consent need to be able to justify their decision, or they may be guilty of assault.

Sterilization and abortion

The days of compulsory sterilization of people with learning disabilities are thankfully gone, but one still comes across women with learning disabilities who were treated in this way in the past. Carers, parents and medical staff may have seen this as a possible solution if there were concerns about the woman's level of understanding of sexual matters, when she was known to be sexually active. These days, the regular contraceptive injections so often used are effectively a less final form of the same approach. Control of a woman's fertility in this way can be to the client's advantage, as long as she knows what the procedure of sterilization (or the regular injection) is for. As before she needs to understand the implications of such a decision and be in agreement. Otherwise the medical practitioner must make the decision, on the grounds that it is in the client's best interests.

While parenthood should be a choice, often a woman will discover that she is pregnant unexpectedly. If this happens, both she and her partner should be made aware that abortion may be an option, and that the decision to become parents is one that is better made voluntarily. There may be religious or ethical objections to abortion, and these also need to be recognized and discussed, both with the client and with parents, families and carers. As with any other medical intervention, clients need to know what the physical and psychological risks may be, and be aware of possible alternatives, including fostering or adoption of the child.

Choosing to be parents

People with learning disabilities, like anyone else, may choose to be parents and make a decision to try and begin a pregnancy. Once pregnancy is confirmed, and the decision is made that the child will be kept, then the parents need to be given support and education to help them provide the level of care that a child will need. These consist of emotional support and advice, basic information and education about childcare, and realistic resources to ensure that the physical and emotional needs of the coming child can be met. As in other spheres of life, this may mean there is a need for regular input from support workers or care staff in order to allow the person with a learning disability to lead as normal a life as possible with their child. Currently it is difficult to obtain more than minimal support in such situations, and too often the child is removed into social services care because lack of resources make it impossible for the mother or parents to have adequate support.

SARA

Sara has discovered that she is pregnant. She and her boyfriend had been having sex on a regular basis, at his insistence, even though Sara had tried to say no. She was not using any contraception, and although initially dismayed about being pregnant, she has decided that she wishes to have the baby and keep it.

Sara lives in her own flat, and has little contact with her family. She is supported by her keyworker, who visits daily, and generally Sara can manage well on her own, although she needs help with budgeting and planning meals. She has little idea of what caring for a child will really mean, but likes the idea of being a mother. If she is to keep her child and care for it she will need considerable daily support, as she is unable to meet even her own needs unaided.

Assessment of risks

RISKS TO SARA

There are a number of health risks associated with being pregnant, including the risks associated with miscarriage, complications of pregnancy, and the birth itself. Sara has some understanding of the birth process, but little awareness of any other risks. She has some expectation that she will get help from her boyfriend, although those who know him well suspect that he will not be interested in providing this, and is likely to abandon Sara.

RISKS TO OTHERS

There are risks to the baby, in that whether Sara decides to have an abortion or to continue with parenting alone will result in different outcomes for the child. There are also possible risks to the child in the future, if Sara is unable to continue parenting.

FREQUENCY

Many of these risks are one-off risks associated with being pregnant and will not be repeated unless Sara becomes pregnant again. However, the risks associated with trying to keep the child and raise it alone will be ongoing and will probably occur daily. The child's health and safety could be put at serious risk on occasions, if Sara does not receive adequate support in caring for her child.

LEVEL OF RISK

Most of the health risks associated with pregnancy are relatively low-level risks, that is, statistically they are rare. Nevertheless they are serious risks and the worst outcome is death, for the child, or the mother, or both. Thus these risks need to be carefully considered. However, it is also worth noting that most women of normal ability take these risks also and would not be deterred from seeking to become mothers by the existence of such risks, largely because, with modern medical techniques, they are now relatively low.

POSSIBLE OUTCOMES

Sara could miscarry, or suffer from any number of complications associated with pregnancy. She could die giving birth. These are all relatively low-frequency risks, but with potentially serious outcomes. In the longer term, Sara may have her child taken from her at birth or later, if she proves unable to look after it. The child may be at risk because Sara cannot care for it adequately, or may not be able to keep it safe once it becomes more active. She may come to feel negatively towards her child if it reminds her of its father, and this would also be a risk for the child. Both Sara and her child could suffer from psychological distress as a result of these problems.

Management of risks

Ultimately, Sara's success in being a mother, and likelihood of being allowed to keep her child will depend upon her level of skills and abilities, her capacity for judgement, and the level of support she receives. The latter is likely to be crucial. Ideally Sara and her child should receive the care they need to remain together. In reality, lack of resources may increase Sara's risk of having her child taken from her.

Assessment of Skills and Abilities

Being an effective parent requires a significant range of skills and abilities. Moreover, these have to develop and change as the child grows. The demands of a small baby are very different from the demands of an older child or adolescent. There can also be difficulties if the child born is of normal ability, and by early teenage years has outstripped its parent(s) in ability level. In assessing skills and abilities we need to consider a variety of areas.

Cognitive ability

This is perhaps the first area that most people will think about. What we mean by cognitive ability is a subject of much discussion, but fundamentally it is a combination of knowledge and problem-solving ability. It also includes a capacity to use these two faculties together, so that old knowledge is applied to new problems.

Many people with learning disabilities can learn new information and skills, although they may need longer to do so than most people. Generally it is their problem-solving ability which is poor, and while problem-solving is a skill which can be taught to some degree, it is harder to teach than more practical skills. However, it is this ability to problem-solve, and to use existing knowledge when new problems arise, that is perhaps one of the most important skills of everyday life, and is particularly so in successful parenting.

Cognitive skills can best be assessed formally by an IQ test, and this should only be administered by a qualified clinical psychologist. Although such tests can be very reliable, there is always some variability in the results, and this can be difficult to interpret for the layman. IQ figures are still only a guide to the level of ability, and the number itself is not the whole story. IQ tests also vary in their format and, as mentioned in chapter 4, different tests may give different results, although the variation is not usually large. However, a psychologist should be able to gain a lot of information from a good IQ test such as the Wechsler Adult Intelligence Scale (WAIS). This will include some information about cognitive strengths and weaknesses, and information about short-term memory, language skills and numeracy, as well as overall IQ.

Knowledge

Much of the process of caring for children simply requires knowledge of how to do it; what to do and what not to do. A client who is going to become a parent needs to be given the time and opportunity to obtain this information in an easily accessible form.

The series I Want to be a Good Parent (McGaw 1995) is an excellent introduction to the areas that need to be covered, and is easy to read and understand. Clients with poor reading skills may need help with these booklets, but they include lots of excellent drawings illustrating the various aspects of childcare, and what is important. Clients may also benefit from opportunities to meet other parents and see how children are cared for, and the chance to meet other parents with learning disabilities can be particularly helpful.

Memory

Although the IQ test may reveal some information about memory function, it may still be worth getting an assessment of memory function as such. Memory is a complex function, and has a number of stages. These are:

- *Attention.* The capacity to attend and concentrate on one thing at a time, and register its content or form.
- *Registration.* The capacity to retain the new information and hold it in the mind for a short period of time to consider it.
- *Retention.* The capacity to remember information for long periods.
- *Access.* The ability to get information back from memory when it is needed.

When memory fails it can be at any of these stages, but for people with learning disabilities the first stage is often a real problem. They may have difficulty concentrating, and thus the information may never get satisfactorily registered in the first place. In day-to-day life, this may mean that they miss important information in the environment, and thereby put themselves and their children at risk. They fail to register hazards, or to hear warnings. They may be easily distracted, and thereby miss things which are important.

Even when information is attended to and retained, people with learning disabilities may have more difficulty than most in accessing the information when needed. They may know what they need to know, but fail to put it into practice at the right time.

Carers can assess these capacities informally, but again a formal assessment of memory by a clinical psychologist may be helpful

The problem of judgement

The capacity which is most difficult to assess formally is judgement. It is a combination of problem-solving ability together with the capacity to assess risk and to make decisions based on one's assessments. Good judgement requires that one can assess a situation and the possible responses to it, and decide on the best or most appropriate response. It is extremely difficult to teach this to people with learning disabilities who do not possess it. However, it is this capacity above all others which appears to determine whether people can be successful parents in the long term.

We all have times in our lives when our judgement might be questioned by those around us: the choice of an unsuitable partner, the time we got drunk at the office party and said the wrong thing to the boss, the time we got caught for speeding, etc. Interestingly, these poor decisions may often (although not always) be made at times when we have been drinking. Alcohol affects the executive systems of the brain, and appears to make us more likely to behave impulsively, that is, to lack judgement.

It is not unusual for people with learning disabilities to have problems which are similar to those of people who are drunk, or who have suffered from brain injury and whose executive functions are consequently impaired. The behaviours which are characteristic include a tendency to take risks, poor problem-solving, difficulty in understanding another's point of view, and a tendency to be more easily moved to emotion than normal. In addition, they are often absent-minded and can appear irresponsible.

Such difficulties all tend to make it harder for them to demonstrate what others would call 'good judgement'. When combined with a lack of knowledge, and possibly also a poor memory, the person with learning disabilities may thus be operating at a significant disadvantage. Not only can these difficulties make it harder for them to cope independently with their own lives, it can make it extremely difficult for them to be an effective parent. Much of the process of child-rearing involves having to judge situations, make decisions, and assess risks. If the person with learning disabilities cannot judge risk for themselves, they will certainly not be able to care for a growing child safely, without help.

Formal assessment of these functions, and thus of the capacity to make judgements, is difficult. While a number of tests of executive function exist, many of these may be too complex for most people with learning disabilities. However, it can be instructive to attempt to administer some of these tests where possible. The results can sometimes clearly illustrate the nature of the problems which the client is encountering in everyday life. Once again, the assistance of a qualified clinical psychologist will probably be necessary here.

Concern is often expressed as to whether tests designed for the normal population should be used with people with learning disabilities. However, this is not as much of a problem as is often suggested. The aim of such an assessment in this context is to determine how well the person with learning disabilities can cope with the demands of the 'normal' world, and as such the standard tests can provide an interesting insight into their difficulties. This is often more helpful than knowing how their performance compares with that of other people with learning disabilities.

On a day-to-day level, care staff and families can often give a reasonable account of how the client can or cannot make judgements about decisions, risks, etc. based on their own observations. It is worth getting into the habit of noting down when clients make particularly good or bad decisions, and the situations which prompt these. Over a period of time such records can be very helpful in building up a picture of how the client functions. Their capacity to assess risk effectively in relation to themselves is particularly important, as stated above. If they are unable to do this safely, they will be unable to care for a child without considerable help.

The implications of providing support to parents

Where cognitive capacity is limited, and memory and judgement are poor, the client who wishes to be parent is therefore at a considerable disadvantage. Not only will the process of learning be slow and difficult, the ability to know when and how to employ any knowledge gained will be also limited. In order to keep a child safe, it is likely that a parent with such difficulties will need almost constant support and supervision to function effectively in the parental role. Current resources are unlikely to provide this kind of support, and, more often than not, the child will be taken into care.

The better the range of abilities that the client can be shown to possess, the more likely that they will be given the opportunity to keep their child and be a parent in the real sense. At present, there does not appear to be much commitment to the idea of supporting parents with learning disabilities to enable them to keep their children wherever possible. The tendency seems to be for social services to intervene by removing the child rather than by providing the necessary support. Largely this is prompted by lack of adequate resources, but it may also reflect an unwillingness on the part of the authorities to accept that parents with learning disabilities can be effective parents. It may be that the impact of the Human Rights Act will ensure that the situation improves, but the resource implications, particularly for social services, are significant.

Particular Problems for Parents with Learning Disabilities

Where parents have managed to keep their child, they are often aware that the price of doing so is frequent interference from those in authority. Most of us are allowed to be parents without constant supervision, and consequently our mistakes, when we make them, are less public. Parents with learning disabilities often feel that they are constantly under scrutiny, and have a sense that the standards expected of them are impossibly high.

The reality is that we have all made mistakes as parents, and that we should allow parents with learning disabilities to do so as well. Of course serious mistakes are not desirable, and if the child's health or safety is seriously compromised then action must be taken. As before, the seriousness of the outcome, and the likelihood of it occurring, must be taken into account when assessing risk. Parents should not be condemned because the home is untidy or not as clean as some would wish. A home has to be extremely dirty to become a real health hazard.

It is worth spending a little time identifying what the important characteristics of the 'good parent' might be. Winnicott spoke of the 'good enough' parent, although his focus was more on emotional than practical care. Nevertheless, the concept of the 'good enough' parent might be helpful here.

Parents need to ensure that small children are:

- well fed
- relatively clean
- warm
- dry
- given the chance to sleep regularly
- loved and cuddled.

Parents need to know how to fulfil these needs in practical terms, and also to understand why they are important. If memory is a problem, written checklists may be helpful to remind them to consider all these areas if the child is distressed and will not settle.

As the child gets older, they also need to be able to:

- keep the child safe (from accidents, abuse, neglect)
- teach the child new skills (e.g. toilet training, eating independently, making friends)

- put limits around the child's behaviour (discipline)
- respond to requests and demands from the child.

The older the child is the more complex these needs become, and a growing child is a challenge for any parent. Teenagers can be particularly demanding, and if the child is more intellectually able than the parent it can lead to real problems. Children soon learn to manipulate their parents, and the learning-disabled parent may be at a significant disadvantage when faced with a wily teenager of normal or near-normal ability! A further difficulty may arise when the child is more able than the parent, in that they become aware that their parent is unable to keep them safe. This may cause an anxious child to become extremely distressed at times.

Mothers with learning disabilities are particularly vulnerable to exploitation by more able partners who may seek such partnerships knowing that they will be able to abuse both mother and children. A mother with learning disabilities may not even be aware that her new 'boyfriend' is in fact more interested in her daughter or son than in her.

In the early stages of parenthood, it is easier to be confident that parents can cope. The child will thrive, grow and gain weight if all is well. Poor hygiene will show itself relatively quickly in a child who always has nappy rash, or stomach upsets. Alert health professionals will soon pick up any such problems, and can intervene. Later, it becomes more difficult, and problems may come to light less easily. Childhood behaviour problems may be the first indication that all is not well. Bedwetting, tantrums or withdrawal, for example, can all be signs that a child is distressed. Once the child is at school, it may be teachers who notice first that all is not well.

There is a fine line to be drawn between the needs of the parent and the needs of the child. While every attempt should be made to allow parents with learning disabilities the chance to be 'good enough' parents, it is also important to remember the needs of the child, and the problems which may develop if the child does not receive the care and protection necessary. Once again, considering the likelihood of a given risk and the seriousness of the possible outcome(s) may help to clarify thinking in this area.

However, we must remember that parents with learning disabilities start out at a disadvantage. Unlike the rest of us, they tend to be assumed to be incompetent without such assumptions being tested out. As long as the child is not at serious risk of harm, they should be given the chance to prove themselves as effective parents, and the standards expected from them should not be greater than the standards expected of anyone else. It is also worth noting that it is now widely accepted that people with learning disabilities can live a much more 'normal' life when they are given the level of support they need to do so. The same should apply to parenting. Even if a mother with learning disabilities needed a constant companion to help her care for her child, it is possible that this kind of support would enable her to experience motherhood with all its joys and trials. What is lacking at present is the will and the finance to make this possible for a significant proportion of such mothers. Removing the child is usually seen as the only option, but it is not necessarily the cheapest one if all the long-term consequences of putting a child into care are considered.

The Need for Support: Helping and Monitoring Care

In the early days of a child's life, his or her progress will be assessed regularly by the midwife, and following that by the health visitor. One of these professionals will often be the first to notice if all is not well. Ideally the assessments carried out before the child is born, as above, will have highlighted areas where there is a need for support. This might result in parents being involved in parenting classes, or having the help of regular input from support workers. In practice, support worker time tends to be limited, and input is often minimal. However, good support workers can be invaluable in assessing the real situation in the home, and alerting professionals to areas of concern. This can be done unobtrusively and without causing parents unnecessary anxiety. Support workers may need additional training to do this effectively, but this is probably a valuable investment in the long term. There are costs involved in taking children into care: this money might be better used in giving families the right level of support, so that they can keep their children at home.

Mother and baby units where parents can be taught and observed while interacting with their children can be helpful in ensuring that they have, and use, the skills to care for the child. Some formal instruction in childcare may be given. However, what is crucial is whether the parent can take these skills back to her own home and put them into practice appropriately. Many people with learning disabilities can learn new skills, but fail to remember to use them in new situations.

Once again there is no real substitute for unobtrusive observations in the real home setting, and support workers are ideally placed to carry this out. Small problems can be nipped in the bud, while larger ones may need to be reported to the professionals who are involved in caring for the parents and child. However, it is important that removal of the child from its parents should be the last option considered, not the first, unless there is clear evidence that the child is in danger.

Areas of concern

In the early days, the child will eat and sleep and do little else. Both midwives and health visitors will monitor weight gain and general development. At this stage, as long as parents are co-operative, there is usually no problem in monitoring the child. However, as it develops and becomes more independent, these services will usually gradually with-draw. For parents with learning disabilities this is often just the time when the child is becoming more demanding and difficult to manage safely.

A mobile child will explore everything, and it is at this stage that a parent with learning disabilities may begin to have problems. Being aware of potential dangers, and taking steps to prevent harm to the child, may be something that they find very difficult. Parents, both learning-disabled and otherwise, often attribute 'wilfulness' to children at this stage, and may be over-zealous in their discipline. Both accidental and non-accidental injuries may result, and even a high level of accidental injuries is a cause for concern. As before, a support worker who is visiting regularly may be in a position to pick this up before anyone else.

Older children, in addition to their need for care and protection, will also begin to demonstrate needs in other areas if the parents are not meeting these. For example, a child who appears withdrawn and unre-sponsive, or is prone to extreme tantrums, is indicating emotional distress, and is trying to communicate this. A child who readily goes to strangers for affection may be lacking it at home. Most normal children are wary of strangers, at least initially. Problems such as bedwetting, nightmares and aggression can all suggest that all is not well. The difficulty is that many perfectly normal, well-cared-for children may also show these behaviours from time to time. In themselves they may only signal a temporary upset, which is not serious. It is important, therefore to put them into context, and monitor them over time.

If the child seems happy, reasonably sociable, responsive to the parents, and is developing normally in physical terms, then there is probably no need for concern. If there are real problems then the child will reveal its distress in a variety of ways, in different contexts. Communication between everyone involved with a family where there is concern about the parents' capacity to cope is essential.

ROGER

Roger is 3 years old. He has significant learning disabilities, as does his mother. His father was of normal ability, but has left the family, and Roger's mother relies on support from her own mother to get by. She lives on benefits and does a little cleaning for a neighbour on the side. Roger is showing some behavioural problems, in that he still wets the bed, and is prone to tantrums when he can't get what he wants. The health visitor is concerned because Roger is significantly underweight for his age, and his speech is also delayed. He has been seen on four occasions at the local accident and emergency department with cuts and bruises, and on one occasion with a badly sprained wrist. The local nursery school, which Roger has just started attending, is concerned because he always seems hungry, is often in dirty clothes, and is aggressive towards other children.

Assessment of risks

RISKS TO ROGER

In the above example, any one of the professionals who might become involved with Roger, although concerned, might not feel that there was a serious problem. A child psychologist might receive a referral to see Roger because of his tantrums and bedwetting, but at 3 years old these are not uncommon. Similarly the health visitor may be concerned about his slow development, but could attribute this to his learning disability and being naturally small. The accident and emergency department may also be somewhat concerned at the frequency of admissions, but may not feel that the injuries are severe enough to warrant intervention at this stage. The nursery school, which is part of the educational system, may not be aware of the concerns of the other professionals, and may not take action even though it may feel worried about the care that Roger is receiving.

If, however, all these agencies get together and discuss Roger's case, then it becomes clearer that there may be a real cause for concern for his welfare. He may be being physically abused, or he may simply be neglected, or both. What is clear when the overall picture is considered is that Roger is suffering in a number of ways, and action needs to be taken.

Risks to others

Roger's aggressive behaviour may put other children at risk.

Frequency

Roger is probably at risk on a daily basis. He appears not be getting enough to eat, and the injuries seen by the hospital, and his aggressive behaviour, suggest that his mother may be being over-zealous in her disciplining of him. At best, she is unable to keep him safe. In addition, his mother seems to be unable to meet his dietary needs effectively. All of these problems are occurring on a regular basis, and the consequence of this frequency is that Roger's health and safety appear to be at considerable risk.

Level of risk

The risk to Roger's health in a number of areas seems to be significant. His rate of growth is poor and he appears to suffer from frequent 'accidents'; these may be genuine, suggesting poor supervision, or they may be non-accidental, suggesting that his mother's approach to disciplining him is unacceptable. His injuries so far have been significant, but not life-threatening. At worst, however, Roger could be at risk of death, or severe physical injury, even though to date his injuries have been relatively minor. At best, he is likely to suffer considerable psychological distress. His failure to thrive may affect his long-term health in other ways.

Possible outcomes (short- and long-term)

Roger could be at risk of serious injury in the short term. It is clear that his mother is unable to keep him safe, and may actually be harming him.

In the longer term his health may be at physical risk from poor diet or he may be at risk of serious psychological problems caused by his maltreatment. Action needs to be taken to protect Roger, and in this kind of situation his needs must take precedence over his mother's, because he may be at risk of serious harm, both in the short and longer term.

Management of risks

It is important to stress here that if the family has a number of professionals or agencies involved it is vital that information is shared between them. Risks may be assessed by each individual professional, and by the care worker, but only by putting all the information together can a clear picture of the child's situation be gained. It is unfair to assume too readily that parents with learning disabilities cannot care effectively for their child, but it is also unfair (and possibly dangerous) for the child if action is not taken when it is necessary. Issues about confidentiality should not be allowed to prejudice the safety of the child.

Nevertheless, it would be better for both Roger and his mother if attempts could be made to discover why she is unable to care for Roger effectively. Children tend to be attached to their parents, however inadequate they may appear to others, and the loss of his mother may cause additional distress. His mother may simply lack knowledge about suitable diet, or effective ways to discipline Roger. Or, if she has this knowledge, she may be unable to make effective use of it. Time spent in a family centre may help to identify the areas of difficulty, and it may be possible to provide the kind of support which will then enable Roger to stay with his mother. However, family centre staff may not be familiar with the problems experienced by mothers with learning disabilities, and may themselves need training and support in this area.

It is also worth investigating whether Roger and his mother are simply reacting to the loss of his father. Both may be distressed by this loss, and if his mother has become depressed it may explain her failure to care for Roger properly. Psychological and/or medical treatment for her may greatly improve the situation.

When Things Go Wrong

The protection of children at risk in the UK is now supported by a clear set of guidelines for both health service and social services staff. If a child is considered to be at risk, then action must be taken to inform social services, who will then investigate. However, this is a highly emotive area, and the judgement of carers, families and professionals can sometimes be less than truly objective. This is one of the reasons that child protection conferences seek a majority view, rather than allowing one professional view to hold sway over others.

Weighing up risk to a child against the distress caused to its parents is never easy. The situation may be further coloured by the feelings of the child, who may resist leaving the parental home even when his or her safety is compromised. This is a very difficult decision for social workers to make. They must weigh up the wishes of the parents, the wishes of the child and the level of risk they perceive. When the child is very young its view of the situation may not be sought, but increasingly, if the child is able to express a view, this will also be taken into account.

Where the concern is around sexual or physical abuse, the picture is perhaps clearer than if the concern is about more subtle neglect or suspected emotional abuse. While the child's view may be relevant, it is worth bearing in mind that a child who has grown up with such treatment will have little awareness that life could be any different. As with people with learning disabilities who have grown up in institutions, they will lack the capacity to make a real choice because they have no knowledge or understanding of the alternatives available.

Trying to avoid serious risks

As discussed earlier, parents with learning disabilities should always have the opportunity to receive education about not only sexual matters and contraception, but also about child development and practical instruction on caring for a child. If parents come to the attention of the authorities later on, it is worth checking that such education has been undertaken at some stage. If it has not, then parents should be strongly encouraged to participate.

Support workers are an invaluable first line of defence, but they need to be mature and well trained, ideally with their own experiences of parenting, so that they have realistic expectations of parenthood. In addition to training, they need good supervision from a professional who has experience of people with learning disabilities, and is aware of the issues around child protection. Good relationships with the parents are essential, and it is important that the parents should not be given the feeling that they are constantly being criticized.

While this all sounds quite straightforward, in practice it may be much more difficult to achieve. Support workers are often hard to get, and they are poorly paid. Training for them is often minimal, and the turnover of such staff can be high. Thus it may be difficult to establish the kind of relationships which ideally will foster co-operation and thus increase the chances of any problems coming to light. Supervisors of support workers need to be aware of these issues, and ready to take steps to minimize disruption, and ensure that support workers feel valued and supported themselves.

In addition professionals who supervise support workers should take the time to meet the clients and get to know them. Unless they have some idea of the home situation and the characteristics of the parents, they will find it difficult to make appropriate decisions about risk and the need to intervene. Equally, however, it is worth remembering that those who spend a lot of time with clients may lose their ability to look at the situation objectively, and their opinions and decisions can be coloured by emotion. Supervising professionals may have the benefit of some detachment from the situation, allowing a more measured decision to be made.

Generally, the best way to assess risk in these situations is to have good knowledge of the client and his or her skills and abilities. Often this will enable the professional or carer to make reasonably accurate predictions of where difficulties are likely to arise. In addition it is important to build relationships based on trust, so that the parents feel able to confide their difficulties to those assisting them. Over-critical and invasive supervision of the parents is likely to breed resentment and secrecy.

Finally, consider seriously the level of risk, and the possible outcomes, as before. If there appears to be a real risk of harm to the child, even where this is not the intent of the parent, then action may need to be taken. Where the likelihood of real harm is very low, then it may not be necessary to intervene, but just to be alert to the situation, and monitor it carefully. The defining factor should be the child and its physical and emotional state. If it seems clear, as in the case of Roger above, that the child is distressed, then action must be taken to protect him or her. This need not, in the first instance, be the removal of the child, but this may be necessary if other interventions fail. If, however, the child seems content, physically fit, and is growing and developing reasonably well (allowing for some degree of learning disability as a possibility), and most importantly, if it appears to be attached to and content with its parents, then a little dirt and untidiness is of no real consequence.

Summary

Parents with learning disabilities do have significant problems which make parenting much more difficult for them than it is for the rest of us. Parenting is a difficult job anyway, especially as children get older, and few of us manage it without making mistakes. What is particularly hard for parents with learning disabilities is that they feel they are monitored and assessed at every turn so that any mistakes they do make are glaringly obvious to all. There needs to be a change of attitude, such that society is willing to provide the resources for adequate support which will enable such parents to experience the joys and sorrows of parenthood as we all do. To deal with the situation by immediate removal of the child does not seem a just response to their difficulties. Of course where the child of learning-disabled parents is truly in danger of harm there is no question that action should be taken to remove it to safety, just as would be the case with the children of any other parents. It is never easy to make such a decision, but careful analysis of the nature of the risks involved may help to clarify the thinking of those who have to make it.

chapter six

SELF-HARM, MENTAL ILLNESS AND RISK

Risks Related to Self-Harm in People with Learning Disabilities

In people with learning disabilities deliberate self-harm is relatively common, especially in those whose language is limited. It is often defined as a form of *challenging behaviour*, a term which in itself is difficult to define satisfactorily. Typically, challenging behaviour is said to be that kind of behaviour which challenges traditional care services. It can range from mild swearing to serious physical aggression or self-injury.

Some types of people with learning disabilities appear to be more prone to indulge in self-harm than others. Those with Lesch-Nyan syndrome, for example, are particularly difficult to deter from their particular type of self-harm, which usually includes biting and chewing of the lips, and there is some evidence that this may be the result of biochemical abnormalities. Most people with learning disabilities who self-harm tend to indulge in head-banging, hitting themselves with their fists, biting or chewing parts of the body (often fingers or arms), scratching themselves, or picking at scabs on existing injuries. Some will throw themselves about violently against walls or windows, or deliberately break windows, cutting themselves in the process. At such times clients often appear unaware, or perhaps uncaring of, the risks to which they are exposing themselves.

The seriousness of the injuries sustained can vary enormously, and some people who indulge in these activities can be relentless, to the point of preventing injuries from healing, and producing ulcers and/or scars. Until recently restraints, helmets and other types of restrictive device were often employed to try and stop such behaviour. In recent years the focus has been much more on trying to determine the reason for the behaviour and attempting to prevent it by other means, or to develop alternative coping strategies for the client.

As a broad generalization, self-harm can usually be considered to be an expression of psychological distress. This is true whether or not the person has learning disabilities. It is often a strategy for communicating, albeit one which may not, to others, seem particularly effective. Nevertheless, it is often interesting to note how effective self-injurious behaviours can be in assisting the client to re-establish some degree of control over their situation. If regular self-harming behaviour begins, or recurs after a period during which it has been absent, the first question to be asked is 'What has changed for this person?'

Much challenging behaviour therefore, including self-harm, is an attempt to communicate distress and engage attention. This does not mean that it should be dismissed as 'attention-seeking'. We all seek attention, and without it we become depressed, and feel devalued. For people of normal ability, attention is obtained from family, workmates and leisure activities with others. We feel that we can have an impact on the world, albeit in a modest way. Many people with learning disabilities do not have opportunities for such experiences, and so-called 'challenging behaviour' may be their only way to get the world to take notice of them, especially if they have little or no language.

Determining the Reasons for Self-Harm

The reasons for self-harm can vary enormously, but most reveal some effort to communicate distress. Changes of various kinds can result in self-harm: a favoured member of staff or fellow resident may have left, or even died. A family member may have died or moved away. The person's daily routine may have been changed, or they may have had to move to another home. Depending on the client's level of ability, it may be possible to talk to them about what has happened, and thereby ease their anxiety or distress. Even clients who cannot talk may often have some understanding of spoken language, and may respond to explanations. Symbols and pictures may also be helpful in communicating with those whose language is limited. Where there is no obvious cause, further investigation may be needed to discover what is going on.

Understanding and Managing Deliberate Self-Harm

If a client is indulging in self-harm, then the first step should be to ensure that, as far as possible, the environment is made safe, and the client is supervised or accompanied. It may be possible to discourage self-harm by distracting the client with other activities, and often just the additional attention will be sufficient to reduce the self-harming behaviour. Given time and patience, the client will usually adapt to any environmental changes or losses, and the level of distress will abate.

However, where there are no apparent changes or losses to account for the self-injury, or the above approaches do not succeed, detailed assessments by a clinical psychologist or a behavioural specialist may help uncover the reasons for the behaviour. Understanding the reasons for self-harming behaviour is essential if it is going to be possible to manage the risks.

Self-harm can also be linked to time of day (night-time is often a particularly frightening time for former victims of sexual abuse, if their abuser used to always come in the dark) or even a time of year. Anniversaries, or occasions when people leave or die, may arouse memories of past distressing events and trigger episodes of self-harm, with or without an associated deterioration of mental health. It may also occur in response to particular types of demand or interaction, or as a response to particular people.

JOE

Joe was prone to bang his head violently at times during the day. He did this so often that he had a permanent bruise on his forehead, and at times a sore would develop. Many of the care staff said that this just happened when Joe was in a bad mood. However, when charts were kept of when and where Joe banged his head, it became clear that he did it whenever someone tried to insist that he did something. However, it was also noticeable that it happened a great deal more with some members of staff than others. When this was examined further, it became clear that if someone asked Joe to do something by saying something like 'Do you fancy a bath, Joe? You could have a bubble bath if you like', Joe was happy to co-operate. If, on the other hand, someone said 'Hey Joe! Time you got in that bath', Joe would resist by banging his head. The important factor appeared to be the tone of voice in which Joe was addressed. If ordered around in a loud voice, he would react by banging his head. It also seemed to be more likely to happen when the request was made by members of staff whom he did not know very well.

Assessment of risks

RISKS TO JOE

Joe is regularly harming himself, and this could be serious if he persists. He already has scars as a result of his self-harming behaviour, and he could do himself more serious harm if his head-banging continues unabated. He has an almost continually sore place on his head from banging it, and it is not unknown for clients like Joe to actually fracture their skull as a result of such head-banging. Even mild brain injury could result.

RISKS TO OTHERS

There are no apparent risks to others.

FREQUENCY

Joe is banging his head at least daily, and often several times a day. This is a very high-rate behaviour, and this therefore increases the risks to Joe.

LEVEL OF RISK

Because of the frequency of this behaviour the level of risk is fairly high that Joe will continue to damage himself. While the likelihood of severe damage is relatively low, the more he bangs his head, the greater the risk of a serious outcome.

POSSIBLE OUTCOMES

Joe could develop a chronic infection, further scarring, or even brain injury as a result of his head-banging. The more frequently that this behaviour occurs, the greater is the likelihood of these more serious outcomes. There is also a risk that he may lose his home if the care staff feel that they can no longer cope with his behaviour.

Management of risk

In these kinds of situations, it may be possible to draw up behavioural guidelines which will record in writing the best way to approach Joe, in order to avoid these kinds of problems. Psychologists called in to advise on behaviour problems will often produce such guidelines, the idea behind them being that all staff will behave in a consistent way towards the client. If this can be done, the likelihood of the unwanted behaviour occurring will be much reduced. In Joe's case it is clear that he likes to be approached gently and politely, and that he is then usually co-operative. Strange staff, or those who are more directive, are more likely to trigger Joe's head-banging behaviour.

Guidelines not only need to indicate the best way to approach to Joe, but may also recommend that any new staff are initially placed on shifts where there is at least one member of staff familiar to Joe. Interactions with Joe could be restricted to this person while he gets used to the presence of the new face. While it may not always be feasible to implement these suggestions, if the guidelines are followed as far as possible it is likely that Joe's head-banging could be much reduced. However, this approach will not work unless everyone agrees to do the same, and to treat Joe in the same way. When the self-injurious behaviour is at a level where the person's health and safety are significantly under threat, it is vital that all staff follow such guidelines to the letter. *It only takes one person to not do so to undermine the whole process.*

In order for staff and managers to feel confident in managing such clients, it is wise to establish an agreed overall plan of care for any client who is prone to self-harm. This will include behavioural guidelines, as well as clear indications of how to deal with situations where the behaviour escalates out of control. As with the example of Joe, it may be enough just to specify a particular manner in which to approach the client. In more serious cases, it may also be necessary to agree in advance with medical staff that alternative medication can be given, and managers need to have a contingency plan in place so that extra staff can be made available if needed. Staff should also note any intervention that appears to help, as well as those that seem to make things worse, so that all care staff are aware of useful and appropriate strategies. If at all possible this should be done in advance of the client's arrival in a new setting, and certainly not left until a crisis occurs. In extreme cases it may be necessary to identify an emergency bed in a secure facility, where the client can be removed if it proves impossible to continue managing them at home. When the level of self-harm is likely to be serious, managers need to be prepared to make extra staff available to offer extra support and supervision to the self-harming clients and his or her fellow residents. Staff themselves may also find these episodes distressing, and need extra support.

Self-harm or attempted suicide

In those with learning disabilities, as in the normal population, self-harm is perhaps more common than genuine suicide attempts. However, for many people with learning disabilities who self-injure, the behaviour will serve different functions from the kind of self-injury more often seen in mental health clients, sometimes called parasuicide (for example cutting of wrists and arms). Where clients do indulge in the more serious forms of self-harm such as cutting or burning themselves, the origins of these behaviours need to be understood. People who have been physically, emotionally, or sexually abused tend to be particularly prone to self-harm, and those with this kind of history often appear to use it as a way to manage their anger, frustration, or low mood.

Various theories have been put forward to explain this, from self-punishment to a desire to obtain care and attention. The behaviour may serve a number of purposes, but one thing is certain, punishment will not prevent its occurrence. At one time, clients in hospitals who indulged in this type of self-harm were immediately secluded in locked rooms, or put into other forms of restraint, ostensibly to prevent them from indulging in further episodes. In practice this could often degenerate into a punitive regime of repeated seclusion, and a battle between the client attempting to continue with the behaviour and the staff who were trying to prevent it. This approach did little to treat the underlying causes of the behaviour.

It is important to realize that this kind of self-harm is *not* attempted suicide, and is much closer to the kind of self-harm seen in those with more severe learning disabilities. It appears to be a way of expressing distress, managing unpleasant feelings, and/or communicating. Consequently it should not be dismissed as 'attention-seeking' or ignored. Strenuous attempts should be made to try and understand the reasons for the behaviour. Understanding will often suggest an obvious way to manage its occurrence, and specialist help should be sought.

Mental Illness

The presence of mental illness can affect both the levels of risk that the client poses to him- or herself and the risks posed to others. There has been considerable debate about the extent to which the presence of mental illness increases the risk of violent behaviour, and it is generally agreed that there is no consistent association between the two. Nevertheless it is known that, in certain circumstances, serious mental illnesses such as schizophrenia, especially where there is a paranoid component to the illness, can significantly increase the risk of aggressive or violent behaviour. This condition is inclined to make people more likely to commit unpredictable acts of violence, which are motivated by the ideas and fears that are in their head.

Generally speaking, however, the increase in risk associated with mental illness is usually the risk to the self. People with mental illnesses such as schizophrenia and depression may be more likely to self-injure, or to attempt or commit suicide. As a group, they are not necessarily more of a risk to others. In people with learning disabilities the presentation of mental illnesses may be different, and it is sometimes difficult to make a diagnosis, particularly with those of lower ability levels. Where clients have limited or no language it can be extremely hard to discover the exact cause of their distress, and sometimes psychosis may be diagnosed when no other explanation for the behaviour can be found.

Diagnosis of mental illness

While a tendency to anxiety is usually fairly easily recognized, the existence of depression is often missed in those with learning disabilities, largely because it tends to manifest itself in physical symptoms as much as psychological ones. People with learning disabilities may be less likely to express their feelings, partly because of language difficulties, and partly because they do not expect that help can or will be forthcoming.

Lack of interest in activities, withdrawal, loss of appetite and sleep problems may all be symptoms of depression and it is important to be alert to the possibility of a psychological explanation as much as a physical one. Risks here are often around self-neglect, such as failing to eat. Suicidal attempts are less common than in a psychiatric population, but may still occur amongst the more able people with learning disabilities. Reckless or extreme risk-taking behaviour can also occasionally be associated with depression.

Similarly, psychosis in people with learning disabilities may be difficult to diagnose. Behavioural problems may provide the first clue that all is not well. There may be an increase in violence or aggression, or sexual behaviour may become disinhibited. As with depression, sleep may be disrupted, and appetite can be affected. The risks may be both to the individual and to those around him or her. As with those of normal ability, psychosis associated with paranoid delusional beliefs can be particularly worrying, as these may often focus on fears of being attacked or harmed in some way. Much of the aggressive behaviour shown by such clients is by way of a pre-emptive strike, to attack others who are seen as hostile. This behaviour can often appear quite unpredictable, and in consequence may pose significant risks to care staff and others who come into regular contact with the client.

In addition, psychosis is often linked to some loss of contact with reality, and this may lead clients to take unnecessary risks themselves, because they are functioning less effectively and failing to recognize risks in the normal way. Even where the client's speech is usually good it may become unintelligible, or difficult to follow, leading to further isolation and confusion. If clients begin to show such changes, it is important to seek psychiatric advice.

Assessing risks in those with mental illness

In assessing risk, it is often more helpful to look at the particular individual and their behaviour, rather than focus on a diagnosis. Schizophrenia or depression, when well controlled by medication, may not be of any real significance in themselves. The way in which symptoms are expressed may be very important in assessing risks, but the key factor here may be whether the person concerned is actually taking their medication regularly. Often problems arise because the client is reluctant to continue taking medication on a long-term basis, and if they stop the subsequent deterioration in their mental state then considerably increases the risk of behavioural problems. Certain kinds of experiences or situations may make it more likely that the person will relapse. A change of home environment, or an increase of stress of any kind is particularly likely to be associated with relapse in someone who is prone to mental illness, and problem behaviour may follow closely.

It is important in this situation to have a good knowledge of the person, what their triggers may be for breakdown, and how their disorder manifests itself in behavioural terms. Each person will be different. For one person, signs of agitation and sleeplessness may be the indicators that all is not well. For another it may be obsessional interest in a particular topic. For a third, extreme withdrawal may be the signal that deterioration is beginning. There is no substitute here for knowing your client well.

MARTIN

Martin is a young man with mild learning disabilities, who lives with his parents. His home life is fairly settled and his parents cope well with his needs. The family members seem fairly content with each other, are regular churchgoers, and there are no obvious stresses. However, Martin was at residential school for some years as a teenager, and while there he was sexually abused by an older boy. This continued for almost two years before it was discovered, and Martin subsequently developed schizophrenia at the age of 18. The content of Martin's delusions centred around the 'sins' he committed by engaging in homosexual activities with this older boy. When these ideas became particularly troublesome he became depressed and agitated by turns, and had difficulty sleeping. His father tried, at these times, to persuade him to go to bed and try to sleep, but Martin became aggressive towards him, and on one occasion actually punched his father. A further problem is that Martin's self-care deteriorated badly when he was disturbed, and he became smelly, dirty and unshaven. Fortunately, Martin responded well to the medication prescribed for him, and these episodes largely disappeared. However, Martin's father then died suddenly, and Martin's mental state deteriorated rapidly. His mother, already distressed herself, cannot cope with Martin. She is worried that he may become violent again and seeks help from her GP to get him into residential care.

Assessment of risks

RISKS TO MARTIN

There are a number of risks present here for Martin. He is evidently distressed by the loss of his father, and this has been a major factor in the recurrence of his mental illness. It is likely that any major life event may trigger a relapse for Martin, as this is a well-recognized pattern in those with psychosis. When he is ill, his self-care deteriorates to a point where he becomes unpleasant to be around, and this increases the risk that Martin's mother and others may reject him.

RISKS TO OTHERS

Martin was aggressive and violent towards his father in the past, when the father tried to insist on him going to bed. There is a chance that Martin's mother may be similarly at risk.

FREQUENCY OF RISK

Martin has been settled for the last two years, and had responded well to the medication. His current relapse is undoubtedly the result of losing his father. It is likely that he will be vulnerable to relapse when faced with any major life stress of this kind. However, generally speaking these are of low frequency. His violent response to his father only occurred once, when he was previously disturbed, and so the risk of this recurring is also probably low.

LEVEL OF RISK

Although Martin neglects himself, this is not of such a degree that his health is at risk. It might be more of a problem if he was living alone, but currently his mother ensures that he is provided with food, and tries to persuade him to bathe and change his clothes. Martin's poor self-care is distressing for his mother, but not dangerous. However, she is worried that he may hit out at her as he did at his father, even though he has never done so in the past and their relationship has always been fairly close. When he did hit his father, no physical harm was done, and Martin has not attempted to hit anyone since. Thus it is probably unlikely that Martin will harm or injure anyone else.

POSSIBLE OUTCOMES

Martin is certainly psychologically distressed as a result of the loss of his father. He may lose his home if his mother feels that she cannot cope any longer. This could lead to a breakdown in the relationship between Martin and his mother. Martin's long-term mental and physical health could be at risk if no action is taken.

Management of the risks

In the short term, Martin and his mother need to be supported in coming to terms with the sudden loss of his father. If this is not done, there is a likelihood that Martin's mother will decide that she can no longer manage Martin at home, and he may have to move into residential care. While in the longer term this may be a suitable goal to consider for Martin, now does not seem the appropriate time to be seeking it.

Both Martin and his mother could benefit from counselling. Martin may benefit from a short-term admission to residential care, where he can have his medication reviewed and receive counselling. This will relieve the pressure on his mother, and ensure her safety if Martin does by any chance become violent. If his mother is not supported in this way, there is a risk that she will insist on long-term care for Martin elsewhere.

Families can often be very helpful in highlighting triggers or warning signs. In Martin's case, his mother was able to tell the care staff that a sign of deterioration in Martin's mental health was that he started to talk about sin, and being a sinner. He was worried that he would go to hell. This could serve as a useful warning sign to those who may be caring for Martin in the future, as they then know that this change in behaviour may signal an impending breakdown. It also very important that those who do know the client well make sure that these triggers and warning signs are documented for each individual. Those who are new to the care of the client must ensure that they read all the documentation available about each client, so that they are aware of possible changes in situation, mood, or behaviour which may signal the onset of problems.

As mentioned earlier, even where violence, aggression and/or self-injury are not the focus of the risk assessment, it is common for those who are suffering from mental illness to neglect their self-care. This can lead to everything from problems with neighbours, infestation with parasites, malnutrition, hypothermia, or even death in extreme cases. Awareness of the early stages of self-neglect may enable those involved in the care of the client to take action before these problems become established. The primary risk here is not to others, but to the client themselves. Once again, there may be a conflict between apparent client choice and the duty of care, and a decision should be made jointly with all those involved in Martin's care, if there is a need to intervene.

Summary

People with learning disabilities who self-harm and/or suffer from a mental illness present similar challenges to those with such problems who are of normal ability. However, the patterns of behaviour shown by the two groups may be different.

Self-harm requires careful management in any setting, although it is perhaps less likely to be associated with deliberate suicide attempts in people with learning disabilities. A careful analysis of the setting, triggers and consequences of self-harming behaviour is essential for effective risk management. Self-harm is usually an attempt to communicate unhappiness, and should not be ignored, or dealt with by punishment. Both speech therapy and psychological assessments should be obtained in such cases, if at all possible.

Diagnosis of mental illness tends to be more difficult in people with learning disabilities, and there are often problems with management because care staff are not trained to recognize or manage it. Risks of harm, both to the person themselves and to others, are then increased. Management of the illness may therefore be crucial to managing the risks, and for people with learning disabilities issues around self-neglect may be particularly important.

In order to manage self-harm, with or without associated mental illness, it is essential to have professional help from both psychiatrists and psychologists. The majority of care workers are not trained to deal with such difficulties, and may find such clients very frustrating and distressing to work with. Where care workers are working with clients who have these kinds of problems, it is essential that they receive adequate preparation, training and support. Without this they will not be able to keep the clients, the public, or themselves safe from harm.

chapter seven

OTHER MENTAL DISORDERS AND ASSOCIATED RISKS

Mental illness is not the only form of mental disorder that may be associated with increased risks, either for the client themselves or for others. This chapter aims to consider some of these other disorders and the nature of the risks they may pose.

Ageing and Dementia

Ageing is associated with a number of potential problems that can affect any of us. These include deterioration of sight, hearing and mobility. All of these may increase the vulnerability of the person, putting them at increased risk and therefore possibly affecting their ability to live independently. Risks in these cases should be assessed in the same way as everyday risks for younger people with learning disabilities.

However, it is important to make the distinction between normal ageing and the onset of dementia. Dementia is associated with a serious decline in mental and ultimately physical functioning, which is significantly greater than that seen in normal ageing. This can considerably increase the risks associated with everyday living.

While many elderly people complain of poor short-term memory, they are usually able to maintain their level of independent functioning in spite of this. In cases of dementia the loss of memory, while gradual, tends to rapidly become disabling, with the person forgetting potentially serious matters such as turning off the gas cooker, or leaving the front door open or unlocked. It should be stressed, however, that this is a loss of short-term memory and concentration, i.e. a problem with monitoring current activities, and retaining new information. Memories from earlier life, and previous skills, will often be preserved.

Other problems may rapidly develop, such as difficulties in finding one's way around, problems with dressing, and even incontinence. Occasionally, the client may develop behavioural difficulties such as aggression, violence or sexual disinhibition. If these behaviours appear in a person who has no previous history of them, then dementia should be considered, particularly if the person is over 50. The peak age for onset of dementia in people with Down's syndrome is 50, and on occasions one may even see signs in those as young as 30. However, other elderly people with learning disabilities can also develop dementia as they age, just as those of normal ability can do.

Typically problems will increase as the person deteriorates, until they reach the point of complete dependence. The rate of deterioration in all cases of dementia is very variable, however, with some progressing rapidly into total dependence, while others may take years to follow the same path.

Diagnosis of dementia

There are several types of senile dementia, of which Alzheimer's is the commonest. The next most frequently occurring type is multi-infarct dementia, which is the result of a series of 'mini-strokes', each of which impairs an area of function. This type tends to show a 'step-wise' type of deterioration, as each 'mini-stroke' takes its toll. In contrast the progress of Alzheimer-type dementia tends to be steadier and more gradual. Other types of dementia are rarer, but the path of deterioration is often similar. Dementia may begin in the thirties, forties, or fifties, especially in people with Down's syndrome, but typically the onset is much later, in the seventies or eighties.

It is probably now well known that people with Down's syndrome are at much greater risk of developing dementia of the Alzheimer's type. Thus any clients with Down's syndrome who are over the age of 30 should be monitored.

However, it is also known that those whose brains function less well as a result of injury are also at greater risk of developing dementia, and there is some evidence that this may also true for those with learning disabilities, who may also have brains that function less effectively than most. Thus it is possible that learning-disabled clients generally may be at greater risk of early onset dementia than the general population.

Similarly, a family history of dementia may increase the likelihood that a client may develop the disease. There appears to be a genetic component in the development of dementia of the Alzheimer's type. If any client develops symptoms which are suggestive of dementia, medical advice should be sought as soon as possible. However, it may be some months, or even a year or two, before a definite diagnosis can be given, because other conditions, such as depression, can mimic the symptoms of dementia, and these need to be eliminated before a firm diagnosis can be made.

The symptoms of dementia and depression can be similar, especially in the early stages. It has also been suggested that depression may be one of the first symptoms of dementia, or a response to the person's growing awareness that they can no longer do the things they used to do. Withdrawal, apathy, sleep problems and increased anxiety can all be symptoms of both conditions. It may only be by observation and the passage of time that it will become clear exactly which is the true problem. It is worth considering whether there have been any major recent life events which might have triggered a depressive reaction in the client. In some cases, especially where the client has little language, a trial of antidepressants may be helpful. This will need to be agreed with the GP or psychiatrist, and a medical consultation should be the first step in either case.

Risk assessment in dementia

The risks associated with dementia are chiefly those that arise from a loss of memory and skills. As the condition develops, the person becomes progressively less able to cope with activities that previously presented no problems. They may lose co-ordination, become increasingly absent-minded and forgetful, and take risks which they would not previously have done. At times they may become confused and disorientated. The difficulty with dementia is that it is not easy to predict its course. As time goes on the condition worsens, and the sufferer loses skills and becomes increasingly vulnerable, but the rate of change can be very variable from one person to another, and the sufferer will have good days and bad days. Risk assessment in this situation needs to be an ongoing process. Changes can occur daily, and with the changes there may be new risks. Clients who could previously go out alone may suddenly seem to have forgotten their road safety skills, or get lost in previously well-known areas. It is important to be alert to the development of such changes, especially in those with Down's syndrome.

It is also important to be aware that the physical deterioration associated with dementia may result in the client having to move to a different care home. This in itself poses further risks: moving to a strange place is associated with increased death rates in elderly, dementing individuals. Ideally it would be in the client's interests to remain in their existing home, with extra resources put into the home while the illness continues. Dementia is a terminal illness, and it is unlikely that the additional resources would need to be provided for many years.

NAN

Nan is a woman with Down's syndrome who lives in a small community home with three other people with learning disabilities. She is 45, and in recent months the staff have noticed that she seems increasingly forgetful. Her self-care has also deteriorated, and where she used to always have bath in the morning and appeared for breakfast looking neat and smart, lately she often appears grubby and dishevelled. One member of staff also suspects she has also become incontinent on occasions. Staff became particularly worried one day when Nan went into the local town to go to the library (something she has often done in the past on her own) and then disappeared. She was found by the local police two hours later, wandering at the far end of town, confused and distressed.

Assessment of risks

RISKS TO NAN

Several risks may exist here. There is obviously a risk that Nan is developing dementia, and this needs to be investigated. She needs to be seen by the GP and possibly referred for specialist assessment. The risks associated with the episode of getting lost could be significant, especially if Nan was confused and disorientated. She could have been run over by a car, or exploited by others who realized her confusion. She could also have been at risk of sexual assault.

Risks to others

There is little likelihood of any risk to others at this stage. However, some people with dementia can become aggressive or even violent during the course of the illness, so that this may need to be monitored.

Frequency

So far this risk has not been a frequent one. In the past, Nan has often gone to the library alone, where she is well known, and has encountered no problems. If dementia is diagnosed, these independent activities may need to be reassessed, as such episodes could become more frequent.

Level of risk

There is a significant level of risk here. It is clear that whatever the cause of Nan's confusion, she was not functioning normally and could readily have put herself in danger by not crossing roads safely etc. She could also be at risk of exploitation or abuse, although these are probably less likely.

Possible outcomes

In the short term, Nan is likely to have been frightened by her experience, and this in itself may make her less ready to go out alone. Similarly others will be more reluctant to allow her to go out unsupervised. Before she is deprived of her independence, however, possible alternative explanations for the episode need to be fully investigated. In the longer term, if dementia is diagnosed, there are huge implications for Nan's future health and care. She will become increasingly dependent and will probably need nursing care towards the end of her illness. Dementia is a terminal illness; she will not recover.

Management of risks

It may be wise to ensure that Nan does not go out alone again, if dementia is diagnosed. A more detailed medical and psychological assessment is needed, however, to try and determine whether there is any other possible cause for Nan's confusion. In the meantime, she may accept company in her trips out of the home, and if, by any chance, she is reluctant to agree to this, it may be feasible for a member of staff to follow her and observe her from a safe distance.

In the longer term, if dementia is diagnosed, carers and professionals will need to devise a care plan which will ensure that Nan's future needs are met, bearing in mind her likely psychological and physical deterioration as time goes by. This may ultimately require a change of home, although ideally this should be avoided if possible. A better solution would be to provide temporary additional care within her existing home. Sadly, those with dementia and Down's syndrome tend to die at an early age.

Head Injury

It is not uncommon to come across clients with learning disabilities whose disabilities arose as the result of a childhood head injury. In order for them to be considered learning-disabled, this injury has to have occurred before the age of 18. These early head injuries may also be relevant to later risk assessment in relation to the adult, because their resultant learning disability is likely to be associated with similar patterns of problematic behaviour to those developed when someone suffers a later head injury.

Any head injury later in life will almost certainly result in the need to reassess risk management for that individual. A head injury can significantly affect the client's capacity to cope independently and may increase their susceptibility to dementia, as described above. It is worth noting that a head injury can significantly affect anyone's ability to cope independently, even where the injury appears to be mild and their physical recovery is good. If the person injured already has a learning disability, the problems may be greatly increased.

Diagnosis of head injury

Head injuries might appear to be easy to diagnose, but often the subsequent psychological and cognitive effects may not be identified as being related to the earlier physical injury, particularly where this appeared to be relatively mild. Accidents involving short periods of unconsciousness are not uncommon, and are often not even recorded by casualty departments if the sufferer appears well enough to go home quickly. Even those admitted to hospital for observation are unlikely to be followed up unless they actively seek help.

The problems which are common after even quite a mild head injury are similar to those encountered in the early stages of dementia, namely poor short-term memory, problems with concentration, distractibility, loss of emotional control, and occasionally aggressive or sexually inappropriate behaviour. It is important to consider the time of onset of such behaviour changes relative to the injury. If they appear fairly soon after a known head injury then the injury is probably the relevant cause. If, however, there is a delay of several months or years this is unlikely and other causes should be sought.

These kinds of difficulties with memory, concentration and self-monitoring are usually called 'executive problems'. They can result in even a relatively able person being unable to manage and assess risks for themselves, and will often mean that the person needs constant supervision and help to cope with everyday life.

Head injury can also result in apparent personality change, or even mental illness. The person may become increasingly irritable, depressed, or unpredictable. They may take greater risks than they did previously. A previously calm and reliable individual may become impulsive, agitated and forgetful. These kinds of changes can affect relationships dramatically, especially close relationships. Partners, carers or families may no longer be able to cope, and alternative care will have to be sought. In terms of risk, this may mean that a client who was previously capable of independent living may no longer be so, and this can have important implications for their home life, whether they live alone or with others.

Risk assessment in people with head injury

In contrast to the risk assessments related to those with dementia, it may be that, as the person recovers from a head injury, the risks become fewer, as they become gradually more able to assess risk for themselves. Nevertheless, it is rare to find someone who has suffered even a mild head injury who does not continue to suffer from some of the difficulties outlined above. As with those with dementia, repeated assessment of risks may be necessary, and it should be accepted that it is unlikely that the person will return to their former level of functioning.

Where the head injury has resulted in the development of socially inappropriate behaviour, such as aggression or sexual disinhibition, it may be necessary to re-evaluate the provision of care, and an alternative place of residence may need to be found. In order to make such a decision, it is important to assess the risks to both the client and those around him or her.

DAN

Dan is a young man with mild learning disabilities. He learned to drive a car when he was 18, but soon after was involved in a serious accident where he suffered a head injury. Although he made a good physical recovery, as time went by, his parents began to notice that his behaviour had changed. Previously, he was a quiet, slightly obsessional young man, who took great pains to keep himself, his clothes and his possessions neat and clean. Although he had difficulty in learning new things, once he had learned a skill he was usually competent, if slow. After the accident, his parents noticed that he became more and more untidy, and kept losing things. He eventually lost his job as a cleaner because he was failing to do the job properly, and he also neglected his self-care, often being smelly and dirty. His mother became worried that his room was a health hazard, as he left bits of stale food lying around on plates, and empty coffee cups which grew mould. When she tried to intervene, Dan became very angry and threatened to hit her if she ever came into his room again.

Assessment of risks

RISKS TO DAN

Dan is showing classic signs of someone who has suffered a head injury, and of whom friends and family will subsequently say 'he's changed'. The risks appear to be both to Dan himself, who is more forgetful and disorganized, and to his family, especially his mother, whom he has already threatened.

Risks to others

As already noted, Dan could become threatening towards others and there is a chance that he may become violent. His immediate family are probably most at risk, but people who have suffered a head injury typically become more impulsive and less controlled emotionally, so that others with whom he comes into conflict could also be at risk.

Frequency of risk

The health risks are present continuously now that Dan has stopped looking after himself or his room. The other ongoing risk to his well-being is that he has lost his job, and the accompanying payment and status of having a job. The risk to his mother, while more serious, is relatively infrequent, and presumably, if she heeds his direction not to come into his room, it may be non-existent. At present the risks to others remain hypothetical; Dan has not threatened or attacked anyone else.

Level of risk

The overall level of risk is not high, although the loss of his job will put him at risk of both financial and psychological problems. The risk to his mother does not seem to be high, unless she continues to try to intervene. Nor is there an immediate risk to others.

However, Dan's behaviour does illustrate the increased emotionality which often puts the head-injured person's relationships and social success at risk. If Dan were to become aggressive or violent to others he could also be putting his freedom at risk. However, at present this risk is small.

Possible outcomes

The immediate outcome is that Dan has no job or income, and his surroundings are becoming increasingly unhygienic. His health may be put at risk. The long-term outcome may be that Dan's parents no longer feel able to care for him, and at worst, if he became violent or aggressive towards others, he could be detained in secure care. If he is not able to obtain and keep another job, which seems probable, he could become homeless, or require long-term care elsewhere.

Management of risk

Unfortunately there is little that can be done to alleviate Dan's condition. It may be possible to offer him counselling to help him understand the consequences of his head injury, but resources for people with head injury are very limited, and the problems may not be recognized by non-specialist services, including the providers of services for people with learning disabilities. Dan's parents may not even make the link between the motor accident and his subsequent behaviour changes, and will therefore not think to pass this information on to others.

While his mother may be able to contain the risk of violence if she does not confront him, there are then the health risks to Dan himself to consider. It is likely that Dan's situation at home will deteriorate, because his parents will not be willing or able to ignore the unhygienic state of his room. This is likely to lead to confrontation and a real risk of violence from Dan.

Any future placement will need to be able to offer Dan clear guidelines for his behaviour, and staff who are able to deal with his aggression and possible violence effectively, as well as providing him with the practical support he needs to remain safe and healthy. It will be difficult to provide sufficient support for Dan's family to enable him to remain at home safely.

Epilepsy

Epilepsy is common among people with learning disabilities. People who have suffered a head injury are also more at risk of developing epilepsy, and this condition carries its own risks. Epilepsy can develop after any injury or illness which affects the brain. It can also be the result of birth difficulties or congenital abnormalities. It is caused by the formation of abnormal areas of tissue in the brain, which disrupt the normal electrical functioning, and the resulting seizures or 'fits' can take a number of forms.

While modern medications for epilepsy can be extremely effective, a proportion of people who are epileptic may nevertheless have seizures from time to time, and this tendency may place them at risk in a number of ways. People who suffer from learning disabilities and epilepsy face increased risks in everyday life.

Diagnosis of epilepsy

Because of the dramatic nature of major seizures, those who develop this disorder are usually diagnosed early in life. However, epilepsy may develop at any age, and some people may have atypical seizures which are less obvious and thus harder to diagnose. Periods of 'absence', or some hallucinations, can be symptoms of atypical epilepsy, for example. Later-onset seizures can be indicative of brain damage related to head injury, brain scarring following brain surgery, the development of a tumour, toxic conditions, or the development of dementia.

With anyone who is prone to seizures it is important to keep a diary of when and where they occur, and to establish if there are particular triggers. Stress typically increases the likelihood of a seizure in someone who is prone to them, and factors such as lack of sleep, lack of food, certain drugs or chemicals, flashing lights (strobes, TV, or games machines) can all increase the risk of seizure in susceptible people.

Many people who are epileptic will show behavioural or emotional changes prior to the seizure. Sometimes they will be aware themselves that these herald a seizure, and frequently this will be noticed by others close to them, even if they are unaware themselves. Those who are less able will find it more difficult to be aware of these links for themselves, and careful observation by others is very important.

Risk assessment in people with epilepsy

If the frequency of seizures is high, it may be necessary to ensure that the person is supervised much of the time, and that potentially risky situations such as bathing, climbing, or even just going out of the home are carefully monitored. For more able individuals, activities such as driving may be forbidden because of the risk to both the self and others if a seizure occurs. If the person works, activities such as operating heavy machinery or climbing ladders may have to be avoided.

The key factor in making such decisions will be the likelihood of seizures occurring. If they are very infrequent then restrictions can and should be minimal. As with people with learning disabilities in general, it may be preferable to allow some risk-taking in order to maintain a reasonable quality of life. Drug treatment for epilepsy should be reviewed regularly, particularly if seizure control is poor.

Where clients do suffer from epilepsy education is again essential, so that they understand the nature of their condition as far as they are able. Where clients are aware of changes in themselves which herald a seizure, it may be possible to teach them to go and lie down somewhere safe as soon as they become aware of these symptoms. Even where this is not possible, it may be easier to put protective limits around their activities if they understand the need for doing so. Sometimes it is possible to avert or reduce seizures by teaching clients relaxation strategies.

MAVIS

Mavis has mild learning disabilities and epilepsy. She was diagnosed as epileptic at the age of 10, and had a large number of major seizures over the next five years. This resulted in some loss of intellectual ability and the development of the learning disability. However, her epilepsy is now well controlled by medication and she is able to live a relatively independent life. She lives in a residential home and has a part-time job at the local shop. Mavis walks to work along a busy main road. A new home manager has arrived at Mavis's home and has questioned whether it is safe for her to walk along such a busy road when she suffers from epilepsy and, as he says, 'could have a fit at any time'.

Assessment of risks

Mavis is at risk of having a seizure, which in turn carries other risks, but as long as she continues to take her medication the likelihood of this happening seems remote.

FREQUENCY OF RISK

Mavis works three days a week at the local shop, and walks to and from the shop each day that she works. This is about ten minutes' walk. Thus the frequency of the risk appears to be high.

Level of risk

Mavis had her last major fit when she was 15. She is now 27. Thus she has not had a major seizure for twelve years. Even though she is considered to be epileptic, it seems relatively unlikely that she will have another fit if her current drug regime is maintained, and nothing else changes. If Mavis did have another seizure, she could be at risk of injuring herself by falling, or perhaps by being run over by a car. She might have her money stolen while she is unconscious, or even be taken advantage of sexually. However, in view of the low likelihood of a recurrence of her fits these consequences seem unlikely, and the level of risk is therefore low.

Possible outcomes

If Mavis did have another seizure then there is a slight risk that she could come to some physical harm, or be exploited while unconscious. However, these outcomes seem relatively unlikely given the long period that Mavis had remained seizure-free, and are not highly likely to happen even if another fit did occur. If she is prevented from walking to work because of these small risks, there is a much greater risk that she will become frustrated and unhappy about the loss of her independence. This could lead to the development of mental health or behavioural problems in the longer term. Overall, Mavis's quality of life is enhanced by allowing her to continue her existing pattern of activities, and the level of risk seems relatively small.

Management of risk

The new home manager may be wise to ask for a reassessment of the risks involved in Mavis's trips to and from work, but overall there does not seem to be any need to intervene, or to change anything that currently happens. It may be necessary to record that the discussions about possible risks to Mavis have taken place, and the reasons for the decision not to intervene being made. However, that should be all that needs to be done on this occasion.

Drug or Alcohol Abuse

Although not strictly a mental disorder, substance abuse is often treated as a mental health issue. People use drugs and alcohol for a variety of reasons. Often the use is purely recreational, as when the average person has a drink after work. Similarly there are those who use drugs, both legal and illegal, to enhance their leisure time. As long as the use of the substances is moderate, and the person is not addicted, this usually causes few problems. Our society is well used to managing the effects of alcohol and nicotine, and for many people the use of these substances is seen as acceptable in moderation. However, for some people their use can become a problem. They become dependent upon them, and use them excessively. This results in increased risks, often to both the user and those around them.

Diagnosis of substance abuse as a problem

Generally concern is expressed when a person uses a substance to the point that their health and/or social functioning are affected. Some might argue that any use of cigarettes (i.e. nicotine) is bad for health, and should be discouraged. While there is no doubt that this is true, many people within the population make the choice to smoke, and regard it as their right to make a choice to do so. They take a risk, which they have chosen to take. If society accepts that it is reasonable for most people to take that risk, it is arguable that people with learning disabilities should have the same right to take that risk.

As a rule, excessive use of alcohol tends to arouse more concern than excessive smoking. This is probably because excessive drinking tends to result in behavioural changes which affect not just the person concerned, but others around him or her also. While there are health risks associated with excessive use of alcohol, it is the behavioural changes which usually cause the problem to be noticed. People may become noisy, unruly, aggressive, violent, or sexually disinhibited after drinking too much. Those prone to offending are more likely to reoffend when drunk. Those prone to aggression or violence are more likely to exhibit these tendencies after drinking alcohol.

Often people who are likely to use alcohol to excess will have a pattern of drinking in response to stress or unhappiness, so that a personal crisis such as the loss of a job or the breakdown of a close relationship will trigger a drinking bout. People who have an unhappy personal history, particularly those with a history of sexual, physical, or emotional abuse, sometimes develop a habit of excessive drinking to deal with the negative feelings that they tend to carry with them as a consequence. They may turn to alcohol as a way of soothing their emotional distress, and ultimately find they cannot cope without it. People with the same kind of history may turn to drug use for the same reasons. Sometimes they may have been prescribed drugs to help with these emotional problems, but ultimately they become addicted to their use, and cannot manage without them. Benzodiazepines, such as valium and librium, are particularly problematic in this respect, as they have been found to be highly addictive.

People with learning disabilities are probably less likely to become addicted to the use of illegal drugs, simply because their usually protected lifestyle means they do not gain access to them. However, those with borderline abilities may fall into the 'wrong company' and be introduced to such substances, and, like the rest of the population, those with psychological and emotional problems are more likely to use these to excess than those whose background is less disturbed.

Assessment of risks in substance abuse

In terms of risk assessment it should be remembered that both alcohol and drugs can affect behaviour, typically by reducing control and allowing the emergence of actions and characteristics that may not be seen in the person's normal state. People with brain injury are often particularly susceptible to the effects of alcohol, and combinations of alcohol and drugs, or different types of drug together, may produce unexpected results. In those prone to epilepsy, drugs or alcohol may affect the person's likelihood of having a seizure. In more able clients there may also be increased risks of offending associated with drug-taking or excessive drinking, in that stealing is a way of financing the habit. The same may be true of those prone to excessive gambling, even though this is rarely considered as a mental disorder.

NED

Ned is a young man with mild learning disabilities who became addicted to glue-sniffing as a teenager. He also likes to drink beer, and will often drink ten or twelve pints a night if he can afford to. He finances his beer-drinking and glue-sniffing by petty theft. In spite of his learning disabilities, Ned is quite 'streetwise' and has been able to avoid major trouble with the police.

However, one night he is caught by the local police after trying to steal a woman's handbag from the bar where he has been drinking. It is soon clear to them that he has been drinking heavily and sniffing glue earlier in the evening. His speech is incoherent and he loses consciousness soon after being arrested. The police discover that Ned has been living in a hostel for the homeless for some weeks. They have to decide whether to prosecute him, let him off with a warning, or refer him for treatment.

Assessment of risks

RISKS TO NED

Ned is obviously not coping well with life, and seems to be in real need of help. His health is being significantly put at risk by his addictions, and he could die, especially as a result of glue-sniffing.

RISKS TO OTHERS

Ned is a risk to others, in that he may steal from them. There is some risk that he could become aggressive if drunk or 'high' on glue, but this has not happened so far.

FREQUENCY OF RISK

On investigating further, the police find that Ned has been using glue and alcohol to excess for some time. The hostel staff have known of him for several months, and he has come and gone quite a number of times over

that period. They suspect that he has been involved with a gang of petty criminals, who have been shoplifting and stealing from cars. It seems that the frequency of Ned's glue-sniffing and alcohol abuse is quite high, and these behaviours are probably occurring daily. The associated risks related to committing petty crimes are probably also occurring fairly frequently – certainly weekly, if not daily. The hostel only see him when he is without money, and while, officially, he is not allowed to use glue or alcohol on the premises they are fairly certain that he does use these substances while he is staying there, whenever he can get access to them.

Level of risk

Ned is putting his health, safety and freedom at risk on a daily basis by continuing to use these substances to excess. There are recognized health risks associated with the use of both of these substances, and both can lead to death if used excessively. In addition, there is the risk of being arrested for petty crimes and the subsequent loss of freedom which may result. Ned is taking these risks daily on many occasions, and thus the level of risk that he will come to some harm is quite high. At present the level of risk to others is relatively low, although a potential for violence cannot be ruled out.

Possible outcomes

Probably the least harm will befall Ned if he is arrested and placed in custodial care. This will entail a loss of freedom, but will probably ensure that he is no longer able to use glue or drink to excess. In terms of his health and long-term safety, this is probably a good outcome for Ned. In the longer term, it may give him the chance to break these habits and establish an alternative and less risky lifestyle. However, as an offender with learning disabilities, he may be vulnerable to abuse within the prison system, and for this reason this may not be the best option for him. On the other hand, custodial care will ensure that others are protected from Ned.

Management of risk

It is clear that if no action is taken, it is very likely that Ned will continue his risky and anti-social activities unchecked. He is unlikely to understand the risks that he is taking at present, and equally unlikely to be able to manage his own behaviour without help. Indeed he probably does not see his behaviour as a problem.

The best outcome for Ned would probably be custodial care in a secure psychiatric setting, where he could be taught about the risks he is taking and helped to find an alternative lifestyle. He will probably need ongoing support and help to maintain this new lifestyle in the future, and to avoid a return to his addictions. The police may need to seek an order for compulsory detention for Ned, to ensure that he obtains the treatment he needs. Overall it would seem necessary for both Ned's safety and the protection of others that he is removed from society, at least temporarily.

Summary

It can be seen from this chapter that, as with mental illness, conditions that affect mental functioning can have an important bearing on the assessment of risks related to the individual. The increased risks may be to the individual themselves, or to those around them, or to both. As already stressed, it is important when assessing risk in any situation to gather as much information about the client as possible, including information about conditions such as those outlined in this chapter.

It is also important to ask the right questions of those who know the client, and it is equally important to record the results of the risk assessment and ensure that they are communicated to all who may come into contact with that client. No risk-assessment process is complete without such information and communication.

It is also crucial to balance the risks to the client against the risks to the community. This is particularly important in those cases where aggressive or anti-social behaviour is concerned. There are times when a more restrictive and custodial approach is needed, not only to protect the public, but also because in the longer term it is probably in the client's best interests too. Ideally this should only be a last resort, but if their behaviour is highly dangerous to others the rights of the client will have to be subordinated to the right of the community to be protected.

chapter eight

VIOLENCE AND OFFENDING IN PEOPLE WITH LEARNING DISABILITIES

People with Learning Disabilities who are Violent

As with self-harm, violence among people with learning disabilities is often defined as 'challenging behaviour' and often serves a communicative function. Where there is little language and thus little capacity for negotiation, violence is often the only way to assert oneself and ensure co-operation from others. The 'challenge' is to carers and the services around the client. It is often a clear message that all is not well, and that the client's needs are not being met. In such situations, the risk of violence can be dramatically reduced when time is taken to identify those needs and adjust services accordingly. Very often, alternative methods of communication can be established, and as long as these work effectively the violence will not return.

Violence, like other forms of challenging behaviour, can also be an expression of distress. This may be a response to changes of home, loss of a favoured member of staff, bereavement, or almost any other unwanted change. Much of this kind of behaviour, and the risks associated with it, can be avoided if time is taken to explain and prepare the client as far as possible for future changes. This needs to be done in a way which is meaningful for the client, and this usually means not just using words. Photographs, drawings and signing can all help a client to understand what has happened, or is about to happen. Where language is used it must be simple and clear, and at a level suitable for that client. Where there is uncertainty about the client's communicative ability and level of understanding, a speech and language assessment can be invaluable. It is also worth bearing in mind that violence can sometimes be a response to frustration, and/or embarrassment, related to the inability to express oneself verbally, even where language is understood.

Clients who have been victims of physical abuse, in addition to possibly self-harming, may use violence more readily than others because they have learned that it is a method that people use to get what they want. This is the result of social learning, and such behaviour can often be improved by teaching the client alternative ways to express needs or gain control of the environment. While violence is frightening to those who are on the receiving end, from the client's point of view it is often a signal that they feel powerless, abused, or anxious. It is an attempt to regain control and exert power.

Violence carries a significant pay-off: people are more likely to give way to, and not challenge, the person who is known to be violent. Some people who feel fearful and uncertain may hide behind a façade of violence in order to hide their sense of inadequacy, particularly if they have been raised in an environment where violence is accepted and even respected as a way of getting what you want. It is not uncommon to come across clients who will be threatening to those who appear uncertain around them, but will behave impeccably when faced with someone who makes it clear they are not frightened by them.

Clients who have a history of using violence in this way need to be handled carefully, and firm limits need to be placed around them. They need to receive the message very clearly that violence is not an acceptable way to behave or to resolve problems. This may require the presence of skilled staff, who are used to handling such clients. Where clients have learned that violence can bring them some degree of status, and the ability to get what they want, such behaviour may be much more resistant to change. In these situations it is vital to ensure that clients can learn alternative ways of getting their needs met, which do not include violence. Clear boundaries and limits must be set on their behaviour, and this may require specialist placement in an establishment where staff are trained in the management of violence.

Any violence carries a risk, and this is a potential risk to both the perpetrator and the victim. In order to manage violent behaviour safely it is essential to record as much information as possible about the client's previous episodes of violence in order to establish an understanding of likely patterns and triggers. It is rare to find people who are randomly violent or constantly so. Usually there are clear patterns, and careful analysis of these patterns can guide staff in future management, and thus minimize risk.

With less able clients it may be enough to ensure that their regular needs are met and, as described above, that other methods of communication are available to them, to avoid further outbursts. However, violent behaviour must not be treated lightly. Others may be put at risk unnecessarily if steps are not taken to understand and manage violent behaviour effectively. A referral to a psychologist may be necessary in order to establish firm and consistent guidelines for the management of violent clients.

Predicting violence

There is a huge literature available about the difficulties of predicting violence. Most of it relates to serious violence and those with serious personality and mental health problems. Very little has been written about people with learning disabilities. Nevertheless, it is often said that the best predictor of future violence is past violence, and anyone with a history of violence needs to be managed with care. This applies to those with learning disabilities as much as to those without. Unless there are very good reasons to believe that major changes have occurred, it is always wise to assume that violence is a possibility, and to take steps accordingly. For example, it is not wise to leave young, inexperienced staff in charge of a man who is known to have been violent in the past. Those who have learned to use violence to get what they want are very good at detecting those whom they can exploit.

As already mentioned, people with a tendency to violence tend to be violent in particular situations, and in response to particular triggers. It is extremely rare to find someone who is violent for the sake of being violent. However, although violence is theoretically predictable, evidence from many studies shows that it is virtually impossible to predict accurately. Often the risk of violence will be overestimated. When it is underestimated, however, the results can be disastrous. For the sake of safety it is probably better to overestimate the risk of violence than to underestimate it. Unfortunately this will often have the effect of limiting the offender's liberty significantly. The civil rights of offenders and potential victims will often be in conflict, and deciding who should take precedence can be a difficult moral choice to make. In most cases the law will assume that the majority must be protected from the minority. It is important that other people are not put at risk unnecessarily for the sake of one violent person. Dealing with habitually violent individuals requires specific skills, and if a client is regularly assaulting others or damaging property, then a detailed risk assessment needs to done, urgently.

MIKE

Mike has recently moved into a community home from a long-stay hospital. Staff at the home are keen to give him a good start, although they are aware that he has a history of violence. However, they all believe that much of Mike's violence was probably a result of the deprived and restrictive environment of the hospital, and they are keen to prove that with sympathetic management Mike's need to be violent will disappear. Initially all is well, but after a few months Mike begins to assault staff, and resists all attempts to control his aggression. After six months, Mike is assaulting staff almost daily. Several staff have left after he has hit them, and morale in the home is low.

Assessment of risk

RISKS TO MIKE

Mike is assaulting staff but not fellow residents. He is therefore at a low risk of being assaulted in return, but he is at serious risk of losing his placement in the community home. This will probably mean a return to secure care.

RISKS TO OTHERS

Mike does not use weapons, but he is a tall, strong young man, and some of the staff he has hit are much smaller than him. He is also inclined to target female staff, and many of the female staff are scared of him. Mike has bruised and frightened several members of staff, and one female member of staff had her arm broken when Mike pushed her over.

FREQUENCY

Mike is assaulting staff every day, and, although not all assaults are serious, there is always a chance that one could be. Thus the risk is occurring very frequently.

LEVEL OF RISK

There is a high level of risk that Mike will lose his home and that he may be moved into a locked facility, thereby losing much of his freedom of movement. The assaults on staff are occurring daily, so there is a fairly high level of risk that a member of staff will suffer serious injury. This also puts Mike at risk indirectly, in that he could find himself accused of serious assault and in trouble with the law.

POSSIBLE OUTCOMES

Mike may lose his home and/or be locked up. At best, his quality of life will be reduced. At worst, he could go to prison, if a member of staff is seriously injured. Staff are likely to leave, and those who choose to remain may suffer serious injury. Staff are stressed and frightened. The home manager could be at risk of legal action for damages if action is not taken to protect his staff adequately.

Managing the risk

It is important in the first instance to try and keep staff safe. It would be wise to ensure that staff work always in pairs, and that vulnerable staff are not left alone with Mike. Violence cannot be ignored, and others should not be put at risk while Mike is assessed. Once staff are in a safer situation, it would then be helpful to gather some information about the assaults. If records of previous assaults are available (as they should be) then it may be possible to discover patterns in Mike's behaviour. For example, is it always the same people who get hit? How do people approach Mike? Does he react differently to different tones of voice, or types of language? Are some times of day more difficult? Is he reacting to change, or to demands being made upon him?

Once again, a behavioural assessment by a clinical psychologist is recommended, in order to see if any patterns emerge. This may allow the behaviour to be managed within the existing home. If, however, there are no obvious patterns, or if Mike is simply exploiting inexperienced staff to his advantage, then it may be necessary to move him to another situation where staff are more experienced in dealing with this type of client. However, in order to be fair to Mike this should not be done without a thorough assessment of current risks, and an examination of all alternatives. Unfortunately, in situations like this there is often a tendency to simply want to 'get rid of' an unruly client, and there can be resistance from some staff when they are asked to consider and modify their own behaviour instead.

People with Learning Disabilities who Offend: How are they Different?

As with the population as a whole, the majority of people with learning disabilities are not offenders, violent or otherwise. When they are offenders, there are often clear patterns of offending, and typically people who offend do so within a fairly limited range, i.e. they steal cars, or become burglars, or shoplift. Although some individuals may commit a range of offences, many seem to 'specialize'. Thus, as with violence, a previous history of offending behaviour may give clues as to the risk areas to consider. People with learning disabilities are more likely to commit petty crimes, as they do not generally have the intellectual ability to plan more complex ones. However, some offenders with learning disabilities may be exploited by more able offenders, who may get them involved in serious offences, then leave them to carry both the blame and the consequences.

Social and personality factors

Offenders generally tend to come from the less affluent sections of society. This may simply mean that better-off and better-educated offenders are more successful at evading capture, or it may mean that they do not feel they have to offend in order to meet their needs. Some offenders seem to offend just for the thrill of getting away with it, and these may be the most difficult to change. There is certainly some evidence that certain types of personality-disordered individuals tend to seek stimulation and excitement, and offending may be a way of achieving this.

Personality disorders are thought to be the result of poor or inconsistent parenting, often associated with various types of abuse. It is very difficult to obtain agreement among professionals about the nature and origins of the various types of personality disorder, and there is a huge literature devoted to trying to define the most serious form of this disorder, psychopathy. Little effort has been made to examine the relationship between learning disabilities and personality disorders. However, it seems reasonable to assume that some people with learning disabilities can suffer from personality disorders just as some people of normal ability do.

Generally, however, people with learning disabilities who offend are more likely to do so because they are simply unaware of society's rules, or because they are confused or unsure as to whether what they are doing is illegal or not. Sometimes they will wish to appear 'big' or, as noted above, will be encouraged by other, more able associates to carry out offences on their behalf. Often this scenario will be associated with a lack of awareness of the seriousness of their behaviour.

Some people with learning disabilities may be impulsive and will act in anti-social or criminal ways simply because the opportunity is there. These kinds of offenders are poor at understanding the implications of their actions, and even though they may later show some awareness of their wrongdoing, this does not seem to carry enough weight to inhibit their anti-social behaviour. In common parlance these people would be seen as having no conscience, or lacking judgement. Such clients are often not malicious in their intent, and can sometimes be surprised and upset at the strength of response their behaviour generates in others. However, where their behaviour includes taking money or goods, taking illegal drugs, or drinking alcohol excessively it can often bring them into conflict with the law. Some areas of sexual behaviour can also lead them into similar problems; these will be examined in more detail in the next chapter.

The role of mental illness in offending

Mental illness can be a predisposing factor, increasing the risk of offending significantly in some groups. This is largely because of the disinhibiting effects of serious mental illness. Such disorders can increase the risk of offending because the sufferer's judgement may be affected by the illness, and they may say or do things which, in their normal state of mind, they would not. Their judgement is impaired, and they may become more impulsive. Control of the disorder thus becomes crucial to control of the offending. This is particularly true where there is a diagnosis of schizophrenia. People with this diagnosis are often prone to irrational patterns of thinking, and those whose illness has a paranoid component are more likely to interpret the behaviour of others as threatening, and respond accordingly.

Other forms of mental illness, such as depression or anxiety, may lead people to drink alcohol to excess or take illegal drugs, and these in turn may lead to offending behaviour. However, it should be borne in mind that mental illness in itself does not usually result in offending. Usually there are underlying social and/or personality factors which increase the predisposition to offend in those who do so when ill.

Dealing with the law

One of the features of people with learning disabilities who offend is that they may have difficulty in understanding not only that they have committed an offence, but also the implications of this for them. The proceedings associated with being arrested, cautioned and detained in a police station are likely to be more than usually confusing and frightening for them. The formal and complex language associated with legal proceedings is particularly difficult for them to follow, and it has only recently been realized how vulnerable people with learning disabilities may be to leading questions. This can result in them making false confessions when put under pressure. It is because of these vulnerabilities that court diversion schemes for people with learning disabilities have come into being. The aim here is to avoid the person having to go to court, allowing them to be dealt with in a more lenient and appropriate manner. This usually means identifying an alternative secure or hospital facility which can offer a bed and some kind of treatment to the offender.

The nature of offences and their context

The assessment of learning-disabled offenders and the nature of the risks they pose thus requires a careful analysis of both the nature of the offence and the context in which it occurred. It is important to have some information about whether similar offences have occurred in the past, and whether there are any known patterns.

Many offenders, whether learning-disabled or not, are more likely to commit offences when under the influence of alcohol or drugs. In these cases it is helpful to be aware of particular patterns of drinking or use of certain drugs which may predispose the person to offending. Frequently such substance abuse will also be a way of dealing with other crises in the user's life. It may be important to be aware of distress arising from any recent changes in a person's life, such as recent bereavement or loss of a job, as this may also predispose them to offending.

In some cases offending will be linked to certain groups of people who are known to incite the person to offending behaviour, or, in the case of sexual offending, access to a particular group of people, such as children, may be the relevant trigger. Violent offending may be linked to situations where the person feels powerless or frightened, or perhaps where they can perceive that they can gain control of the situation by using violence. A knowledge of the person's history can be helpful here: some people will only be violent towards people of a certain age group, race, or sex.

It is important to stress here that sometimes the kind of information discussed above will simply not be available. It is also important to realize that *lack of information does not necessarily mean a lack of risk*. Where there is a lack of information, others involved in the care of the person should be made aware of this lack, just as they need to know what information *is* available. This is particularly important when there are a number of different people involved in the client's care, or there is a change of personnel or home. In some settings it is not uncommon to have clients brought in from the street by police officers, when very little is known about them. It may even be difficult to establish their true identity in the early stages of detention. This makes any kind of detailed risk assessment impossible. In such circumstances it may be wise to assume the worst, and be over-cautious rather than put others at risk.

Looking at previous history: frequency, patterns and opportunities

When assessing risk related to offending of any kind, the following issues need to be considered, and efforts made to obtain any missing information if at all possible. The following checklist may be helpful in gathering relevant data:

1 Has this person committed any previous offences?
2 What were they – are they all of a similar type?
3 How often have offences been committed?
4 Is there a sexual component to them?
5 When did the offending behaviour start, e.g. at what age?

6   Have offences continued throughout the person's life?
7   Have there been times when there has been no offending? What was different then?
8   Do offences happen at a particular time of day, month, or year?
9   Do offences occur in any particular setting?
10 Do offences occur when the client is with a particular person/people?
11 Are there any obvious triggers?
12 Is there any history of mental illness?
13 What kind of mental illness, and what is the nature of the symptoms?
14 Are there any particular ideas or beliefs expressed that could be linked to offending?
15 Is offending linked to taking alcohol or drugs?
16 If there is a victim, is there is any obvious similarity between this victim and any others?
17 Has anything else affected offending behaviour?
18 Has the client any awareness of wrongdoing?
19 Has this awareness had any effect on previous offending?

Generally speaking the longer the history of offending, the more continuous it has been, and the earlier it began, the greater the risk of future offending will be. Offending which is linked to particular situations or people may be avoided by avoiding those triggers. Offending linked to mental illness may be avoided by ensuring regular and adequate treatment of the illness. Careful supervision and control of the environmental factors associated with offending can often dramatically reduce the incidence of offending behaviour. Lack of opportunity will often mean a lack of offending for people with learning disabilities.

It can be seen from the above list that assessment of risk in offenders is a detailed and time-consuming process. It cannot and should not be done quickly and superficially. There may be managerial pressure to carry out risk assessments, but any tendency to turn these into purely paper exercises must be resisted. Not only is it misleading, but it can be positively dangerous. If care staff doubt their own ability to carry out such assessments then professional help should be sought.

NEIL

Neil has been in trouble with the police for following women. He lives at home with his elderly mother, and spends a lot of his day hanging around the local supermarket. As a teenager, he was diagnosed as schizophrenic, and he still takes regular medication. Neil would like to have a girlfriend, and his ambition is to be married like his older brother. He hopes that by spending time around the supermarket, where there are lots of young women, he will find a girlfriend. If he sees a girl he likes, he follows her home to find out where she lives. Over the next few weeks, he then puts notes through the letterbox, and leaves small gifts of chocolates or flowers on the doorstep. His 'victims' find Neil's behaviour very disturbing. He is known in the area, and is often chased by gangs of youths as a sex offender. Neil has been frightened by these experiences, but still continues to follow young women. He fails to realize that by following them, often talking to himself, he appears threatening, not friendly.

Assessment of risks

RISKS TO NEIL

Neil is at risk of being arrested by the police, beaten up by local youths, or assaulted by one of his 'victims' or a member of their family. Because of his odd behaviour he is considered to be threatening or dangerous by many members of the local community. He is also at risk of being locked up, either in hospital or in prison, because local people believe he is a sex offender, and blame him for any offences which occur in the area.

RISKS TO OTHERS

To carry out this assessment properly, it is essential to know if Neil has ever harmed anyone. Does he have a criminal record? Is there any record of him actually touching his 'victims' or does he simply follow them? Is he more likely to follow women when he is more psychologically disturbed? Does medication help? What kinds have been tried? Is Neil co-operative about taking it? Does he have any understanding of how his behaviour is seen by others? Does he understand that he may be at risk himself?

On the face of it, his behaviour, though alarming, appears harmless. However, more information about Neil's history is important before this decision can be made with any confidence.

FREQUENCY OF RISK

Neil is at the supermarket most days. He is therefore at risk very frequently. Similarly, if any risk is identified for his potential 'victims' then they are also at risk very frequently. This frequency means that the level of any risk identified is fairly high.

LEVEL OF RISK

Investigations have revealed that Neil does not physically harm his victims in any way; he has never touched any of them. However, he has badly frightened one or two of them. Overall, therefore, the level of risk to others is low. Nevertheless, there are also significant risks in this situation to Neil himself, who may be beaten up or locked up if he continues with his current behaviour pattern.

POSSIBLE OUTCOMES

Neil may cause a great deal of psychological distress to his chosen 'victims'. He is also putting himself at risk of physical harm from other members of the community who do not trust him, and believe that he is dangerous. Consequently he is at risk of being locked up, either in hospital or prison. The latter outcome will also put him at risk of exploitation of all kinds, and this could result in further deterioration of his mental health.

Management of risk

Neil may benefit from treatment aimed at helping him understand how others perceive his behaviour. It is also clear from talking to his mother that he is more likely to follow women when he is most psychiatrically disturbed. Thus a review of his medication, and careful monitoring to ensure that he takes it, may improve the situation dramatically. A further intervention would be to attempt to provide Neil with alternative daytime activities, so that he is occupied, and perhaps has more appropriate opportunities to meet women who may be willing to consider him as a possible boyfriend. Often a relatively simple management strategy like this can be the most effective in controlling offending or anti-social behaviour in people with learning disabilities.

The Role of Supervision and Management

The legal system has two models of offending, neither of which is really very helpful when considering people with learning disabilities. In the first model, the person who offends is seen as evil and in need of punishment. The notion is that punishment will deter them from offending again, and they will have 'learned their lesson'. In reality this does not work very well with offenders of normal ability, and there is little evidence that it is an appropriate model for offenders with learning disabilities.

In the second model, the offender is deemed to be 'sick' in some way, and therefore not responsible for his or her actions. Although this is closer to an appropriate model for people with learning disabilities, it is still not really suitable in that 'sickness' implies a temporary condition, which a learning disability is not, and also that there is likely to be a 'cure' at some stage. In reality there are problems with both these models when applied to the normal population, and they certainly do not serve the needs of people with learning disabilities very well.

Usually the most effective way of avoiding future offending by a person with learning disabilities is by careful and effective management. As discussed above in relation to Neil, the removal of opportunities can be a great help in avoiding temptation. However, it is not always easy to remove all temptation, and other factors, as already discussed, may affect the likelihood of offending. A certain amount of risk-taking may be necessary if the person is to have any quality of life, and this is where care staff may find themselves confronted with difficult decisions.

It is also important to examine any action that can be taken to minimize the likelihood of an offence occurring. As with Neil, the use of medication for those with known mental illness, or the avoidance of certain types of location or situation for those who are known to target particular types of victim, can help to minimize risks. Good supervision is often the key to success in such situations, and this often does not need to be of a particularly high level to be effective. A good working relationship with a supervisor who is aware of the offender's history can often avoid a variety of problems.

GEORGE

George has a long history of stealing and gambling. He enjoys playing fruit machines, and will lose large amounts of money if not stopped. He has been known to lose £100 in one evening, and when he runs out of money he is not averse to stealing other people's money to continue with his addiction. On several occasions he has stolen money from friends' pockets, bags and purses when they have been left unattended. George knows he should not do this, but seems unable to stop himself, and appears to have little understanding of why the victims become so upset and angry with him. George's stealing has resulted in the loss of jobs and friends on many occasions, yet he does not seem able to change his ways, even though he says he wants to do so.

Assessment of risks

RISKS TO GEORGE

George is at risk of losing all his money, either by his own actions, or as a result of exploitation by others. He is also at risk of being accused of being a thief, carrying the additional risk that he will be arrested and charged with theft. Even if he were to be diverted from court, so that he does not run the risk of going to prison, he may still be locked up as a consequence of his actions. At best he may lose all his friends.

RISKS TO OTHERS

George's victims are at risk of losing their money. However, George is not aggressive or violent.

Frequency of risk

George is likely to steal or gamble whenever he has the chance, if he is not prevented. If not supervised, this could be every day, and in the past has been several times a day. Thus the risk is occurring very frequently, and George is soon likely to find himself in trouble with the law.

Level of risk

Because, if left to himself, George will steal or gamble several times a day, the level of risk that George will lose all his money, steal from others and ultimately get into trouble with the law is high. This therefore means that the risk of his being locked up and deprived of his freedom is also high. However, George is not violent, so the level of risk of actual harm to others is low.

Possible outcomes

George may lose all his money, and if he steals regularly he is likely to lose all his friends, and probably his home too. (He does not distinguish between friends and others, but will steal from anyone, even members of his family. Consequently his family want little to do with him.) George could also fall foul of the law, and at worst could end up in prison. Even if he is placed in a hospital setting instead, there is a very high risk that he will lose his freedom.

Management of risk

Currently George is working in a sheltered workshop, where the manager is well aware of his problems. He keeps a very close eye on George, and everyone who works there has a locker where they keep their money and valuables while at work. The manager has made it a strict rule that no money is left in pockets or overalls, but must be locked away while people work. Similarly, George's care manager is well aware of the problem and his present home has a similarly strict arrangement over the management of money. George is still allowed to go to the pub once a week and play the fruit machines, but he is limited to taking £10 and, when that is gone, he cannot gamble any more. George complains about this regime, but he has to admit it has stopped him from stealing and from losing all his money.

Keeping the offender appropriately occupied and engaged can thus be crucial to effective risk management. This may require an intensive programme of supervised activities, both work-related and leisure-based, but this can still be an effective approach, even if, like George, the offender is of the impulsive, opportunistic type. Where the offender has been unsure of social rules, or has behaved inappropriately for other reasons, as with Neil, regular rehearsal of what is and is not acceptable can be helpful. This does not have to be done in a punitive manner, but simply as a way of reminding the offender of the correct behaviours and the likely consequences if these are not maintained. Group or individual social skills training can be helpful.

THE USE OF PROBATION ORDERS

While some offenders may respond to the more formal approach taken by the Probation Service, for many offenders with learning disabilities this service will not be able to offer the level of supervision needed. Furthermore, probation staff are not trained to deal with people with learning disabilities and may feel reluctant to take on such clients. Thus probation may not be the most effective option for people with learning disabilities.

Ideally this close supervision can and should be provided by care staff, family members, or those involved in the provision of employment or other daily activities. If this is the approach adopted it is vital that all involved parties are aware of each other's roles, and that relevant information is shared freely between them. Failure to share information in such situations is likely to result in unnecessary risks being taken, and a potentially serious or dangerous outcome.

The Courts and the Penal System in Relation to People with Learning Disabilities

For people with learning disabilities who offend, the usual process of the law is often not appropriate or suitable. In law, the model of the 'normal' offender is that someone commits an offence, is punished and thereby sees the error of his ways, and does not offend again. In reality, of course, the situation is very different. Many offenders are not 'normal' in the sense that they often represent the most underprivileged strata of society.

Mental illness is common, and many of these offenders repeat their offences many times.

People with learning disabilities have additional problems, and are especially vulnerable, particularly if they are sent into the ordinary prison system. Court diversion schemes aim to find a more humane and effective way of dealing with such offenders.

Court diversion schemes

Offenders with learning disabilities may have limited understanding of wrongdoing, and their reasons for offending are often quite different from those of other offenders. Once arrested, they may have difficulty understanding the language used by the police and in court, and if they do get sent to prison, as noted above, they are prey to all kinds of exploitation.

The result of concerns about these factors has been the development of the court diversion system in the United Kingdom, where people arrested by the police on suspicion of having offended are assessed by someone with experience of people with learning disabilities. Where it is suspected that the person has such a disability, the professional making the assessment, usually a qualified community nurse, will seek to find alternative ways of dealing with the offender. This may mean arranging for them to be admitted to a hospital or secure unit and/or ensuring that they are adequately protected in any legal proceedings which may be taken against them.

The person with learning disabilities has a right to have a 'responsible adult' with them at all times. This must be someone who can act as their advocate, and ensure that their rights are protected. This person must have an understanding of the difficulties that people with learning disabilities may face when they have to deal with the legal system.

People with learning disabilities in court

Where people with learning disabilities do have to go to court, one of the problems is that they are frequently dismissed as unreliable witnesses. This can prevent them obtaining justice when they have been the victim of an offence, or it can prevent them defending themselves effectively against the accusations of others.

While research has shown that it is perfectly possible for a person with learning disabilities to be a reliable witness, as with children, certain precautions and procedures need to be followed to enable this to happen. At the present time, it is difficult to get the legal system to take people with learning disabilities seriously, although the recent UK government white paper, *Caring for People* (March 2001) does acknowledge the need for change in this area.

People with learning disabilities need similar allowances to those made for child witnesses, because, like children, they may not understand the proceedings of the court, or even fully understand why they are there. Currently, only minimal allowances are made for such offenders, although it is increasingly recognized that if the justice system is to be fair to people with learning disabilities changes need to made, as they have been for children. Special allowances are needed in terms of the language used, the training of legal personnel, and the facilities provided for people with learning disabilities to give their evidence to the courts.

Problems with lack of accountability

With some offenders, this failure to be dealt with seriously by the courts can cause difficulties of another kind. Certain kinds of sex offenders with learning disabilities, for example, may learn that the authorities do not take their offending behaviour seriously, and find that if they select their victims from amongst the most vulnerable learning-disabled people they can continue offending with impunity.

In such situations, if the legal system cannot or will not take action it is imperative that all vulnerable people are protected, and action is taken in other ways to stop or limit the offender's behaviour. In recent years there has been increasing recognition of the need to have formal procedures in place to protect vulnerable adults, as well as children. Usually this will require the offender to be moved immediately to another location, where there is no easy access to vulnerable victims, while assessments are carried out to determine the best long-term course of action.

Summary

It can be seen, therefore, that people with learning disabilities who offend, whether violently or not, need to be assessed and treated differently from more able offenders. While many would argue that the existing system is far from fair or adequate in its treatment of so-called 'normal' offenders, it appears to be particularly unsuitable for those with learning disabilities. They are discriminated against by the legal system, and are belittled or ignored as witnesses. In some cases, the failure of the legal system to acknowledge their particular problems results in some offenders exploiting it to their advantage. More commonly, however, the needs of people with learning disabilities are ignored by the legal system, and they suffer in consequence.

Being labelled an offender, and having to face and cope with the processes of the law, can be extremely difficult and traumatic for a person with learning disabilities. Care staff and professionals have a duty of care to the individual to minimize or prevent offending as far as possible, as well as a moral responsibility to protect other members of society from victimization. The care of a person who is known to be an offender must include regular reassessment of risks, both to offenders themselves and to the likely victims.

People with learning disabilities who offend can change their behaviour, but generally speaking they need help and structured support in order to do so. This is a far more successful approach than trying to punish unwanted behaviour with prison sentences or fines. From the point of view of risk assessment and management, this is also a far preferable approach. By increasing opportunities for useful activity, and ensuring opportunities for unwanted behaviours are limited, the risks associated with offending will be greatly reduced. Wherever possible, offenders with learning disabilities should be offered alternatives to prison, even if these still have to be custodial. With the right kind of input, and good supports in place when they return to the community, much offending behaviour in people with learning disabilities, whether violent or not, can be relatively easily contained.

chapter nine

SEX OFFENDERS WITH LEARNING DISABILITIES

Sexuality in People with Learning Disabilities

Sex offenders with learning disabilities present particularly challenging problems when it comes to the assessment and management of risks. As discussed previously, the majority of people with learning disabilities have for many years been considered as asexual, or incapable of sexual activities. The appropriate expression of sexuality is still a problem for many. In consequence, people with learning disabilities have often had difficulties in knowing how to behave appropriately in relation to sexual matters. They have often lacked not only opportunities to develop into sexually active adults, but also any opportunity to receive even the most basic sex education.

Many of those who have lived the majority of their lives in institutions have suffered from lack of privacy, lack of respect, and often from sexual and/or physical abuse from both other residents and from some staff. Sadly, large institutions seem always to have attracted a small but unsavoury minority of staff who use their position to exploit and abuse vulnerable people. In addition, the large size of many institutions, together with the low staffing levels, has meant that those residents who were inclined to bully and exploit other residents also could have free rein. For those who could not defend themselves, victimization was a significant risk. For these clients sexuality is likely to have become associated with fear and pain, and it is particularly difficult for many of them to see sexual behaviour as potentially enjoyable.

Expressing Sexuality in Socially Acceptable Ways

Even where sexual experiences have been less traumatic, people with learning disabilities have frequently missed the normal opportunities for sexual experimentation as youngsters. Lack of privacy may mean that their sexual behaviour has been confined either to toilets or to deserted outdoor locations. Alternatively, some of these former inhabitants of institutions may appear disinhibited, masturbating in public places, or in living-rooms, simply because they have never had the opportunity to learn more appropriate patterns of behaviour. This can sometimes result in clients being labelled as 'sex offenders' because their sexual behaviour is inappropriate solely as a result of ignorance.

In clients such as these, public masturbation is a relatively common problem, as is inappropriate touching. Often these 'offenders' can be easily managed by simple instructions to limit their sexual behaviour to their own rooms, and clear messages about what is acceptable behaviour and what is not. Firm and clear attempts should be made to redirect their behaviour, for example by teaching that masturbation in one's private bedroom is acceptable, while masturbation in the living-room is not.

Personal care undertaken by a provocatively clad young woman may well result in 'inappropriate sexual touching' by her male clients. In these situations, managers may have to counsel staff about dress codes. Care staff need to be clear about what rules they are trying to enforce, and be relentlessly consistent in doing so, if problems are not to recur. Management of risk here is about teaching both staff and clients what is required, and ensuring that responses to inappropriate behaviour are consistent.

Some people with learning disabilities, however, will show more persistently anti-social patterns of sexual behaviour, and will consistently engage in behaviour which is likely to place them in conflict with their fellow citizens, and ultimately the law. Care staff looking after such clients have a duty to identify behaviour which is unacceptable to the community at large, and to take steps to prevent, or at least limit, its occurrence. This is necessary to protect other residents, care staff themselves, and the public from such behaviour, and to protect the offender from possible police attention and/or prosecution. In addition it is not acceptable to expect fellow clients or staff to tolerate sexually offensive or abusive behaviour on a regular basis.

In practice, of course, it is often very difficult to prevent inappropriate sexual behaviour. The sexual drive is very strong, and the need to express sexuality is a recurring one. If inappropriate sexual behaviour persists, it may be helpful to refer to a clinical psychologist for sexual assessment and education. A risk assessment could also be part of this assessment procedure. It may be possible to produce behavioural guidelines that will assist care staff in managing the behaviour more successfully, and thus reduce risks to all.

In assessing the risks around inappropriate sexual behaviour it is essential to assess the client's level of sexual knowledge, as well as to build up a picture of when and where such behaviour occurs, and what are the possible triggers. Where the sexually inappropriate behaviour is particularly worrying, such as when it centres around children, for example, it may be possible to manage it by simply ensuring that the client does not have access to children, or to places where they are likely to be, at least not without supervision. It is probably not possible to suppress the undesirable sexual interest, but it should be possible to prevent its inappropriate expression.

Where sexual behaviour is persistently abusive and harmful to the recipients, it may be necessary to take steps to remove the client to a specialist residential setting where they can be closely monitored. Sometimes this will require legal intervention, such as sectioning under the Mental Health Act. Once again the assessment of risk, using the criteria outlined in earlier chapters, may be helpful.

Consider the following three men, all of whom might be called 'sex offenders'. The risk criteria outlined earlier are used in assessing the risks around each of them.

BERT

Bert is 64 and has severe learning disabilities. He has always been known to 'like the ladies' and will cuddle up to female care staff who know and like him. His new keyworker is 24 and wears tight T-shirts and short miniskirts with black stockings. She is a curvaceous, friendly young woman and Bert says that he likes her very much. One day she approaches the home manager, very distressed, and says that Bert keeps grabbing her breasts while she is helping him wash and dress.

Assessment of risks

RISKS TO BERT

Bert is at risk of being labelled a sex offender because of his inappropriate behaviour. It is possible that continuing with this kind of behaviour may put Bert at risk of losing his home. In addition, some care workers may refuse to work with him.

RISKS TO OTHERS

It seems unlikely that Bert intends any harm to his victim. However, he appears to have frightened and distressed her, and he may do this to other young women.

FREQUENCY

Bert has done this five times since his new keyworker arrived. Prior to that he had not done it for a long time. He used to have a young female keyworker some years ago, and one of the older staff remembers that she left because Bert kept 'touching her up'. However, he has not done it to anyone else, and he is never a problem when taken out on trips or visits.

LEVEL OF RISK

Bert's keyworker was shocked and embarrassed, but he has not caused her any physical harm. Nor has this happened very often. While the episodes may have caused her some psychological harm, Bert does not appear therefore to present a high level of risk to others. There is moderate level of risk that he will be labelled as a 'sex offender' somewhat unfairly.

POSSIBLE OUTCOMES

These may be that the keyworker is reluctant to continue working with Bert, and may even leave. Other female workers may also begin to feel at risk from Bert, and avoid him. The long-term risk is that Bert becomes labelled as a 'sex offender', and is thus at risk of victimization and/or losing his home.

Management of risk

While the overall risk of serious harm is small, this young woman has nevertheless found this experience distasteful, and she may be discouraged from working with Bert, or indeed other people with learning disabilities. However, the evidence does not suggest that Bert is a persistent sexual offender. He has only behaved like this on two sets of occasions over several years. Rather, the pattern of his behaviour suggests that he is responding to certain cues that the young women with tight clothes are providing. In the absence of these cues his behaviour is not a problem. If young women are encouraged to keep their more revealing clothes for leisure time the problem will probably disappear. The situation needs tactful handling, but if the behaviour is allowed to continue unchecked, then not only will Bert acquire an undesirable reputation, but female staff will be reluctant to work with him. Neither of these outcomes is in his best interests.

Worrying Sexual Interests

Some people with learning disabilities may have clear sexual preferences which others find alarming or disturbing. It is important on these occasions to make a distinction between behaviour which is actually risky or dangerous and behaviour which, while undesirable in some respects, does not harm anyone else.

MICK

Mick is 56 and he likes little girls. He has a large collection of pictures of little girls, often in their underwear, which he has collected from magazines and catalogues over the years. He enjoys watching children's TV programmes, and his favourite outing is to the local playground, where he will sit and watch the children playing. Mick's new keyworker is shocked to discover him masturbating in his bedroom, surrounded by lots of his pictures. Another member of staff says that he is convinced that Mick masturbates when he is watching the children at the playground. As a result of these discussions the staff at the home become very worried, and ask for Mick to be assessed. They wonder if he should be moved to a more secure home.

Assessment of risks

Risks to Mick

How much of a risk is Mick's behaviour? If he has a long-term sexual interest in little girls, this is likely to be a well-established sexual prefer-ence, and very resistant to change. If he has got to the age of 56 without getting into trouble with the law, this suggests that the behaviour is not a problem in the legal sense. There is no evidence that he has ever approached or assaulted a child. However, he does like to observe them, and may gain sexual pleasure from masturbating while he does so.

Mick could be at risk of being labelled a sex offender and victimized in consequence. At worst, he could be accused of a sex offence and find himself locked up in a hospital or even in prison. At best he may find that care staff are critical of him, or may avoid him altogether because of their own distaste for his preferences. Some might even be abusive to him.

Risks to others

In spite of Mick apparent liking for children, there is no real evidence that he acts out any of his fantasies. His pictures are enjoyed in the privacy of his room. The suggestion that he masturbates in the local playground is more worrying, but once again there is no evidence that he approaches or harms the children as a result. The risks appear to be more likely to himself, if he gets caught doing this.

Frequency

There is not much evidence about the frequency of Mick's masturbation while looking at his pictures in his room. However, the fact that he has collected them for many years suggests that this is probably a long-term pattern of behaviour that probably occurs fairly regularly. Mick visits the playground about once a week.

Level of risk

Although many people would find the idea of Mick masturbating while he watches little girls play somewhat unpleasant, the fact is that he does not seem to present any risk to the children in so doing. Thus the level of risk is low. There is no suggestion that the children have any awareness of Mick or what he is doing.

There is a rather greater risk that Mick himself could get into trouble, either because adults with the children may notice what he is doing and assault him, or because they report him to the police. If he is labelled as a sex offender Mick could encounter problems both in the local community and in relation to his current or future placement.

POSSIBLE OUTCOMES

Mick presumably gains some sexual satisfaction from his activities. However, there may be less desirable outcomes of his visits to the playground, as suggested above. Even though many people would deplore his use of pictures of children during his masturbation in his room, in fact this activity is a very low-risk one. Mick gains sexual satisfaction, and nobody is harmed by his actions. The biggest risks would seem to be to Mick himself, not because of what he actually does, but because of what it means to others.

Management of risk

Some would argue that Mick's sexual interest in children is unhealthy and should be stopped. Perhaps he should be deprived of his pictures. However, there is a risk that if this course of action were taken, Mick might develop alternative ways to satisfy his sexual needs which would be more troublesome. At the age of 56 he is unlikely to be persuaded to change his sexual preferences, and he has presumably spent a large part of his life indulging his fantasies and not getting into trouble with the law. If his behaviour was going to progress to more worrying manifestations, it would probably have done so by now. Using his pictures to satisfy his sexual needs is not harming anyone else, least of all the children, and it could be argued that this activity may be protecting local children from harm, by satisfying Mick's sexual desires.

On balance, therefore, Mick's behaviour can be seen as a low-risk behaviour, and probably best ignored. It may be prudent, however, to stop his visits to the playground, especially unaccompanied ones. Staff may wish to discourage any further opportunities for observation of, or contact with, children, but removing Mick's pictures is probably not wise.

More Worrying Behaviour

Some people with learning disabilities, however, are real sex offenders, and display all the undesirable features of these kinds of offender. They will target vulnerable victims, and indicate by their behaviour that they are well aware that they should not be doing what they are doing. They will hide their activities from others, and choose times and places when they will not readily be detected. Such people are dangerous, with or without a learning disability, and the risks should not be underestimated.

TOM

Tom, who is 45, has a moderate learning disability and has lived all his life in a hospital for people with learning disabilities. The hospital closed recently, and Tom was moved into a small residential home. All the other residents are male, as are the staff, because Tom has a history of sexually assaulting women, especially the care staff who worked with him. In the past he has attempted to rape one of the staff in the hospital, trapping her in a large walk-in cupboard. Her screams brought another member of staff to her aid and Tom ran off. Tom doesn't see a problem with his behaviour, although he knows it gets him into trouble at times. In the hospital he would bide his time, and wait until he could get a female member of staff on her own. When he was placed in the home, it was on the understanding that there would be no female staff working there, and that Tom would not be allowed out on his own. However, the new home manager thinks that people are worrying unnecessarily about Tom. Nothing has happened for the last two years, and the attempted rape was five years ago. He is considering appointing a female member of staff because he is having difficulty recruiting males.

Assessment of risks

RISKS TO TOM

The problem with offenders like Tom is that once they are placed in a situation like his current home, where further offending is very difficult, the assumption is often made that the behaviour has disappeared and is no longer a problem. However, sex offenders are notoriously resistant to change, even with active treatment, and it is very unlikely that Tom's behaviour towards women will have changed spontaneously, particularly as he did not really think that it was a problem. What has changed is that he no longer has the opportunities that he used to have.

The risks to Tom are mainly around the possible loss of his new home and, if he does reoffend, that he will be locked up, in a secure hospital or, at worst, in prison.

RISKS TO OTHERS

It is clear from Tom's history that he is a risk to women. Sex offenders are notoriously difficult to treat, and recent 'treatment' of Tom's behaviour has been simply to prevent him having any opportunities to offend. While this can be very effective as a management strategy it does not cure the problem, and if opportunities return it is extremely likely that Tom's offending behaviour will also return.

FREQUENCY

At present, of course, Tom's sexual attacks are prevented by the situation he is in. In the past, his assaults on female staff were very frequent, two or three times a week. They ranged from grabbing a woman's breast to the rape attempt. Often these attacks were quite violent and the victim would suffer at least bruising as a result. It is likely that if female staff were employed in his new home the frequency of Tom's assaults would be as high as before.

Any assessment of the frequency of the risk of offending must take into account the opportunities to offend, or lack of them, that people such as Tom currently have. It cannot be stressed too strongly that while absence of opportunities may control offending behaviour, it will not change the underlying motivation to offend.

LEVEL OF RISK

Tom has been a persistent offender for many years. He was notorious in the hospital, and many of the female staff were afraid of him. His behaviour is unlikely to change at this stage of his life without active intervention, and even then he is not a good prospect for treatment, because he does not see his behaviour as a problem. He causes actual physical harm, and the attempted rape suggests that he might try to rape another woman if the opportunity arose. His victims are also likely to suffer psychological repercussions from being raped or sexually assaulted. Just because Tom has not had any opportunity to rape recently, it cannot be assumed that the risk has diminished. Sex is a recurring need, and sex offenders are therefore the most persistent type of offender. Tom presents a high level of risk to his potential victims.

POSSIBLE OUTCOMES

There are potentially negative consequences for both Tom and any possible victim. If he is convicted of rape, or even attempted rape, he may face a prison sentence. This could put him at risk of victimization himself, as well as losing his freedom. Any victim is likely to suffer bruising at best, and considerable physical or psychological harm could result from sexual assault, attempted rape, or actual rape. In the longer term there is also a risk of pregnancy or disease for a possible victim of rape.

Managing risk for Tom

From the above analysis it is clear that Tom is a high-risk client. However, the key to understanding the level of risk here is the acceptance that *Tom's current behaviour change is the result of a safe environment* rather than of any change in Tom himself. Given the right (or wrong) circumstances, Tom is likely to once again revert to his assaults on women, and his past history suggests that these will be serious, violent assaults, which occur regularly unless he is closely supervised.

Deviant sexual behaviour is particularly difficult to manage and requires expert advice. Assessment and treatment by a clinical psychologist are recommended. This kind of situation requires consideration of two kinds of risk – risk to possible victims, and the risk to the offender that he (or she, but most commonly he) will fall foul of the law. By definition, if he is unable to understand the consequences of his offending behaviour, then staff around him have a duty of care, in effect, to protect him from himself. In such cases, management is best achieved by ensuring that Tom is maintained in a safe environment where opportunities to offend are simply not present.

The home manager should be strongly persuaded against hiring female staff who would without question be vulnerable to attacks by Tom. In the case of clients like Tom, who have a lengthy history of offending, it is vital to have access to as much information as possible about previous offending, and to ensure that any new home or staff group are aware of the likely risks.

Victim or Victimizer?

In some situations it is far from clear whether sexual behaviour can be defined as inappropriate or abusive or not. During the process of caring for several clients, it may emerge that two people with learning disabilities are engaging in sexual activity. Where one or both parties may have a severe learning disability, it is essential that some understanding is obtained of whether the relationship is consenting. As discussed earlier, this may not always be easy. However, as a general rule, where there is inequality of ability level it is reasonable to assume that there is a risk of victimization of the less able partner by the more able one.

Becoming aware of potential victimization

It is important to be aware that differences in ability level may operate in both directions. Males can exploit females of lesser ability, but equally females can exploit males of lesser ability. Convention tends to make it easier to perceive the first, rather than the second type of situation. The past history of each person can be helpful here. Have they had previous sexual relationships? With whom? Were these relationships equal or was there a previous suspicion of exploitation? Who initiates sexual contact? Is it always the same person? Does the other person appear distressed, or wary when around their partner? Have others complained of victimization by this person? Does the dominant partner bully other people? What do the couple actually do?

It is not uncommon for care staff to condone a sexual relationship which is abusive, either in law or in reality, simply because they do not assess the situation in the way described above. Not only is the vulnerable partner being put at risk, but, as already stated, the care staff themselves may be at risk of prosecution if they do not take action to assess and deal with the situation.

Dealing with abusive situations

It is worth noting that many people with learning disabilities, especially those whose experience is of institutional life, have little idea of what constitutes abuse and what does not. They may have little idea of what a reciprocal sexual relationship might be, and consequently will not readily identify a situation as abusive for themselves.

However, where it is felt that there is significant risk of an abusive or illegal relationship action must be taken to resolve the situation as soon as possible. As with situations of child abuse, it is *not* appropriate to move the person who is identified as the victim. The offender should be separated from the victim as soon as possible, and removed elsewhere. Unless it is possible to monitor the situation very closely indeed, they should not remain under the same roof.

Both parties should be assessed fully to determine their understanding of sexuality and sexual behaviour, and the associated risks. Where it is felt appropriate to take legal action, the police should be notified. However it is vital that the victim understands what is being done and agrees to it. There is a very real risk that the victim may be effectively re-abused by the legal process and the need to describe what has or has not been done to them. Where the victim is of low ability, with little language, it is likely that the legal system will not take his or her evidence seriously, and it may not be in the victim's best interests to pursue this course of action.

Similarly, if the abuser is also of limited ability they may be unable to understand the significance of their behaviour, and even if it were possible to obtain a conviction, this would probably not be the most helpful way of dealing with this type of offender. As with all cases of sexual abuse, the victim's wishes should be sought and respected as far as possible. However, if legal action is sought and fails, the victim may be more distressed than if it had never been considered. The primary need is to reduce all risks as far as possible and offer protection to those who need it.

Minimizing Risk of Future Sexual Offending

Minimizing the risk of future sexual offending is far from easy. Sex is a strong motivator, and the sexual urge recurs frequently. Consequently sexual offenders generally are notoriously difficult to treat. Offending behaviour patterns tend to be persistent and resistant to change. While this is also undoubtedly true of some learning-disabled sex offenders, there is a wider range of unacceptable sexual behaviour in people with learning disabilities, which may become labelled as 'offending', but which has quite different origins. Some aspects of this behaviour will be much more amenable to change than others. In many cases, basic sex education, together with some social skills training and clear messages about what is acceptable and what is not, can work wonders.

Where deviant patterns of behaviour are more persistent, it is less easy to reduce risk. The only effective solution is likely to be consistent and firm supervision, with clear boundaries, which, as far as possible, remove opportunities to return to offending behaviour. 'Cure' for sex offenders is relatively rare, and requires a great deal of motivation and persistence on the part of both therapist and offender. For those with learning disabilities this level of commitment to change may be impossible. Good management, and a structured programme of care, in an environment which restricts access to possible victims, may be the only realistic solution. Knowledge of the offender's patterns of offending behaviour and likely victims are particularly important here in order to enable the right limits to be maintained. Those offenders whose understanding of their behaviour is very limited deserve help in protecting themselves and others from their undesirable tendencies. This should be part of the duty of care of those who look after any potential offender.

Problems with the expression of sexuality are frequent when working with people with learning disabilities. Often these are related to lack of knowledge, both in terms of what is appropriate behaviour and what is not, and also a basic understanding of what sexual relationships mean to most people. In some cases problem sexual behaviour can arise simply because of ignorance and curiosity. Wherever sexual problems arise with a client, it is worth making sure that they receive basic sex education as a first step. The following checklist may be helpful in assessing risk and determining an appropriate course of action:

1   What has the offender actually done? (e.g. 'indecent exposure' may simply be choosing to urinate in an inappropriate place)

2   Have they done this before, and how often?
3   Where does the behaviour take place?
4   Is it always in the same place, or same type of place?
5   Who is/are the victim(s)? Are they similar in any way?
6   Is there evidence that the offender knows the behaviour is wrong?
7   Does the offender try to hide their sexual activities, or lure victims to quiet places?
8   Are there any previous convictions for sexually inappropriate behaviour?
9   What is the offender's level of sexual knowledge?
10 Do they have any experience of normal sexual relationships?
11 Do they understand the social and emotional rules associated with sexual behaviour?
12 Do they show any evidence of guilt or remorse for what they have done?

On the basis of this information it should be possible to assess the risks inherent in the particular situation as highlighted in the case studies discussed earlier.

- Consider who is at risk: the client or other people, or both.
- Consider also the *frequency* of the behaviour that is a problem, and where it occurs. (The more frequent and widespread the behaviour, the bigger the problem, and the greater the risk that it will recur.)
- Consider the *level* of risk posed: how much harm is likely to result if an offence takes place? Risks, both to possible victims and to the offender, need to be considered.
- Consider the *possible outcomes*, both short- and long-term, for both victims and offender.

This process should give you a clear picture of the nature of the risk that you are assessing. This should enable you to define a strategy for *managing the risk*. The higher the level of risk, to either offender or victim, the closer the level of supervision and control that will be needed to maintain the safety of all concerned. Where the level of supervision required seems to exceed the capacity of the existing home placement, then urgent consideration needs to be given to moving the client to a more appropriate location.

Summary

Sex offenders, whether learning-disabled or not, pose particular problems because they do not follow the rules of sexual behaviour laid down by society. This causes anxiety and anger at best, and physical and emotional harm to others at worst. Perhaps more than any other area, the issues around sexuality raise emotions, and this makes it doubly difficult to make rational and dispassionate judgements. Serious decisions about the management of sex offenders should not be made by any single individual, and all those involved in the care of the potential offender need to be consulted.

However, it is very important that even when offenders are seen as vulnerable people with learning disabilities, the safety of potential victims is not neglected. In providing suitable care for a potential offender, it can be easy to lose sight of the need to protect possible victims. Equally, at times the needs of victims will be given precedence, and the needs of the offender, who may also be genuinely vulnerable, may be overlooked.

It is also important to understand that, with many sex offenders with learning disabilities, the key to successful risk management is in management of the environment, to limit opportunities for offending. Sex education, and education about what is acceptable behaviour sexually and what is not, can also be extremely important in helping the offender to manage his (or more rarely her) behaviour more appropriately. Good support is also vital. Effective risk assessment needs to consider the needs of, and potential risks to, offenders, their carers and the wider society. This should then point the way to more effective management of any risks.

chapter ten

ASSESSMENT OF RISK WITH YOUR OWN CLIENTS: THE WAY FORWARD

The Lives of Your Clients: What Do They Include and Why?

In order to fully appreciate the process of risk assessment, it will be helpful to identify in your mind one particular client with whom you are currently working. Consider the kind of life they lead at present. How much choice does that person currently have about everyday things? Can they choose when to get up? What to wear? What to eat? When to eat it? How much choice do they have about how they spend their time, and who with? How much choice did they have about where they live, and who they live with? Can they leave the house whenever they wish?

It is very likely that when you begin to ask these questions about your client you will become aware that much of what happens to him or her is determined not by their own choice but by other factors. Compare this with your own life. If you ask the same questions about your own life, how much difference is there in the replies you give?

Having made this comparison, consider why your client has less choice than you do (it will almost certainly be the case that this is so). In some cases, the reasons will be practical ones: social services fund the placement in a given type of home, and there is limited availability. Inevitably this limits clients' choices of where they live. It also means there is little opportunity to choose fellow residents. Lack of choice in eating and sleeping will also be governed by having to meet the needs of several residents rather than just one. The client may lack skills, and have to depend on others to help them dress, eat, or leave the home.

However, it is also likely that, at some stage in the analysis of your client's situation, the question of risk will arise. For example, making tea and toast means exposure to the risks of dealing with boiling water and electricity. Leaving the home unaccompanied is associated with the risk of crossing the road, and possibly having to deal with strangers. Clients are seen as lacking in skills and as vulnerable. Consequently they are protected by being prevented from taking these risks. The overall effect is to severely limit their freedom of choice and scope to be independent.

However, there may also be other reasons for the restrictions placed upon the client. Are they inclined to wander? Have they any road sense? Are they sexually promiscuous, vulnerable, or dangerous? Do they have medical conditions which may make them particularly vulnerable, such as epilepsy? Do they have any history of offending, or is there even a suspicion that they have offended? Is there any concern that they might behave inappropriately while out in the community?

Safety versus Freedom: Who Decides?

Everyone has to make choices between risk and safety. For most of us, this happens so many times a day that we have virtually ceased to notice. Usually we make the decisions about activities that concern us alone. For most adults, it would be unthinkable to allow others to make them for us. Yet most people with learning disabilities have many or all of their decisions made for them.

Many people find that they are subject to more controls and less freedom when they are at work. There are often rules about time-keeping and dress codes, as well as restricted times during which one can take meals. While these may be resented, they are usually accepted as the price to pay for having a job. However, if the same kinds of restrictions were present at home, most of us would be somewhat rebellious! Yet many people with learning disabilities still have to live lives which include these kinds of restrictions, both at 'work' (whatever that comprises) and at home. Even those who are lucky enough and able enough to live in their own flat will often suffer restrictions relating to the tenancy and the kind of support they receive.

Well, you may say, that is all very well, but I can look after myself. My client cannot, and if he or she was allowed the same kind of freedom and choice that most of us have they would be at risk. They would do something silly or dangerous, without realizing the risk involved. It is my job to protect this person, and that is why I have to limit their freedom.

However, consider how you would feel if someone took over your life, and announced the following:

You are overweight. Tomorrow you are going on a strict diet, which will last indefinitely. You will give up smoking; it is bad for your health. You will only be allowed to drink on one evening a week, and someone (anyone) will come with you, to make sure that you don't drink more than two pints. Your taste in clothes is awful, and so from now on your keyworker will choose your clothes for you. You may be allowed to choose one or two things, but going shopping on your own is out of the question. You are already overdrawn at the bank, and you spend far too much money on clothes and alcohol. Your money will be looked after by your keyworker and you will be given £10 a week to spend. The rest will go towards your food, which will be bought for you (because of the diet), or saved on your behalf.

This may paint an unreasonably grim picture of life in a community home, but it is not too far from the reality that many people with learning disabilities have experienced until quite recently. Many still do. The most disturbing aspect of this picture is that all of what is being proposed could be defended as being 'for your own good' and to protect you from yourself. The regime described above would ensure that you were protected from the risks of overeating, drinking too much alcohol, overspending and appearing in clothes which other people thought were unsuitable for you. You would also end up with more money in the bank and no overdraft, as well as slimmer and fitter, if this regime were continued for any length of time. Surely this has got to be in your best interests? Yet how many of us, offered this as a way of life, would see it as preferable to our own? We would resent the interference, and would feel that the right to take risks and make our own mistakes was a vital part of living our own life.

The truth is that we deny many of our clients the same right. Think about your client again. Is this true of them? To what extent has the desire to protect them from risk resulted in a limited and sterile life? Who decides that they cannot take risks and make mistakes? Is this reasonable? Can it be changed, and if so, how?

Defining Problem Areas

As already stated, the price of freedom and choice is risk. Where could freedom of choice be increased for your client, and what additional risks would be involved?

Once again, it would be of value to discuss these risks with co-workers and the client's family. However, it is worth remembering that the families of clients with learning disabilities are often also very cautious about allowing the client freedom to take risks. Moreover, they no longer have the legal right to intervene. For the sake of courtesy they should be consulted, but if their opinion is in the minority they may be outvoted.

As a starting point it may be helpful to list the strengths and weaknesses of your particular client. Where are the areas of vulnerability? When problems occur, what kind of problems are they? Define exactly the nature of the risk involved in any given choice, and decide, using the criteria already outlined, *who* is at risk, what the *frequency* and *levels* of risk are, and what the *possible outcomes* may be. Make sure that you include both short- and long-term outcomes, as well as positive and negative ones. A lot of activities which involve risk-taking can also result in the development of greater independence, maturity and personal growth.

At each stage, consider how you could increase choice for your client while still keeping the risk at an acceptable level. What is an acceptable level? This is difficult to answer outright, but a yardstick to use might be to decide if this is a level of risk that you would accept for yourself or a member of your family.

Making Decisions

Who Decides? (1997) is the title of a recent UK government consultation document which looks at choice, risk and consent for people with learning disabilities and other vulnerable people. It was followed by another, called *Making Decisions* (1999). The aim of these documents was to consult with those involved in the care of people with learning disabilities and advise on the best way to make decisions about their life and future care when the individuals involved were unable to do so themselves. Advice was also given on how this might be undertaken. There has been an important shift in thinking in recent years. The onus is now on professionals to prove incapacity rather than on the client to prove capacity. In other words, a person is assumed to be competent to make their own decisions unless there is good evidence to the contrary. Inevitably this also means allowing people to make mistakes.

However, as discussed before, this has to be balanced against the 'duty of care'. This is where the yardstick 'Would I accept this level of risk for myself or a member of my family?' can be helpful.

Try and define on paper the following:

- What is the choice being made?
- What are the likely risks and *to whom*?
- How *frequently* are the risks likely to occur?
- What is the *level* of risk? (i.e. How much harm can result?)
- What are the *possible outcomes*? (long-/short-term; good/bad)

1   Discuss these with everyone concerned with your client. Then think about any special problems that need to be considered as well. Does this client have any special problems or difficulties which might increase the level of risk for him or her? Can anything be done about these?
2   Try brainstorming possible solutions with colleagues. Don't reject any idea as useless at this stage – just write them all down – then work through them one by one, to see if any of them are workable.
3   Come up with a strategy for managing the risks and associated problems which will enable your client to have more choice in this area. Don't forget to include a plan to deal with the worst possible outcome that your plan allows.
4   Set a time after which you will evaluate progress. Depending on the activity, this might be a day, a week, a month, or even a year later.

Using 'Risk-Assessment' Forms or Not?

Once decisions related to risk-taking and risk management have been made, it is extremely important that these are recorded and communicated to all involved. It must be clear that a formal process has been undertaken, and where the client really cannot choose for themselves, those responsible for making the decisions have done so as fairly, reasonably and safely as they can. In making those decisions, it is almost certain that some risks will be taken. The reasons for taking them, and the possible outcomes, must all be recorded. Some possible outcomes will be so serious and likely to occur that they cannot be countenanced.

However, some may be considered, and if the level of risk is thought acceptable the chance will be taken. However, there should be contingency plans in place. Care staff need to know what to do if the worst does happen.

Typically risk assessment in most organizations requires the completion of a form, as the formal record that risks have been considered. However, risk assessment is a complex process and needs to be done carefully and thoroughly. It requires thought and skill. The difficulty with many so-called 'risk-assessment' forms is that they are often a response to a management directive that 'risk assessments must be done' and are more geared to demonstrating that the action has been taken, rather than truly assessing risk.

Where forms are simply checklists of areas to be considered, there is a danger that lack of information (and thus empty spaces on the form) is taken to mean there is a lack of risk. Furthermore, the completion of the form is seen as an end in itself, and once it is finished the 'risk assessment' is seen as having been done, and the form is filed away and forgotten about. As discussed in chapter 1, risk assessment needs to be ongoing. Although some risks will change little, many can change daily, and any system used should have a review process built into it.

A further problem is that a checklist, while alerting the assessor to areas that need to be considered, does not allow for consideration of the interaction of various risk factors. It is this interaction which makes risk assessment so difficult, but at least if this dimension is acknowledged there is a chance that the decisions made will be more appropriate, and more defendable.

It can be seen from these comments that I am not a fan of risk-assessment forms. However, they can be helpful in identifying the areas which need to be considered. The difficulty seems to arise when people come to see the form as an end in itself, and fail to see it as a guide to a process. It is more helpful to think in terms of a risk-assessment procedure, where those undertaking the risk assessment are guided through a series of decision-making processes. This is what this book has attempted to do, by defining a series of areas which need to be considered. While it is very important to record any decisions and management strategies which are agreed, the use of a single form is not, in my opinion, the best way to approach the task.

If you are in an organization which insists on the use of a form for risk assessment, the best way of dealing with it is probably to use the process outlined in this book to assist in completing the form. It may then be useful to attach another piece of paper with further details of your risk-assessment meeting and the decisions made. You are then in a position to audit both processes, and feed back any results to your managers. Hopefully, over time, you will be in a position to challenge the blanket use of any form which does not prompt people to think carefully about the process of risk assessment.

The Aims of this Book

The aims of this book have been twofold. The first aim is to assist care staff and professionals in the difficult, complex, and often daunting task of assessing risk for their clients with learning disabilities. This is increasingly demanded by management, yet there is a growing climate of litigation and criticism which makes those charged with the task more and more concerned about 'getting it wrong'. By its very nature, risk assessment entails the chance that things will go wrong. The aim of risk assessment should be to ensure that the most dangerous and damaging outcomes are avoided if at all possible, but that wherever feasible clients are given freedom and choice in their lives, even when some degree of risk is entailed. Good procedures for risk assessment can demonstrate that decisions to take risks have been made thoughtfully and with due consideration of all the factors involved. Thus when things do go wrong, which they inevitably will from time to time, it can clearly be demonstrated that this is not the result of negligence, nor a failure to appreciate the duty of care.

The second aim if this book is to enable people with learning disabilities to have fuller lives with greater freedom of choice. This will only happen if those responsible for their care feel confident that they can make the right decisions on their clients' behalf without putting the clients, themselves, or their careers at risk. While there is no absolutely foolproof system for assessing risk, it is hoped that this book will assist those charged with the task to feel more confident and competent to attempt to do so.

The book has attempted to consider various areas of everyday life, as well as the more specific challenges presented by those people with learning disabilities who have other problems, such as mental illness, a history of offending behaviour, or particular conditions which result in increased risks. Assessing risk is complex, but it is not impossible. What is impossible is for our clients to have anything approaching a normal life without taking risks of some kind.

Communicating Decisions

Risk assessment is useless unless the results are shared with everyone who is involved in the care of the client. While it is important to record decisions about risk formally, for the protection of both the client and the staff making those decisions, it is also important to realize that any decisions made will affect the way in which the client should be managed. Where the safety of others is a significant part of the risk, it is vital that such risks are made known to all who come into contact with him or her.

In a community home, both staff and other clients need to have some awareness of the risks posed by a particular client. This can pose problems ethically, because other clients may not be tactful or circumspect in what they say. There is a risk that the client in question may become a victim, if fellow clients then avoid or harass him or her. In these situations, it may be helpful to have rules in existence which, for example, do not allow residents into each others' rooms, when there is a fear that one client may victimize others. Such rules are not ideal, and of course limit the freedom of fellow residents as well as that of the high-risk client. However, at times, the need to minimize the risks to all may necessitate such a move. A risk-assessment procedure in this type of case should consider all possible alternatives and try and decide on the least restrictive way to minimize the risks for all.

When clients spend time in other settings, such as workplaces, day centres, or other social centres, it is important that the staff should also have information about risk, and the agreed strategy for minimizing it for any particular client. Ideally such staff should be part of any group which carries out a risk assessment and devises a plan of intervention for the client. There is a fine line to be drawn between the need for confidentiality and the need for information to maintain safety. As a general rule, the safety of the majority should hold sway over the rights of the individual.

Monitoring Outcomes and Reassessing Risk

It may be that, after the completion of a risk assessment, a decision is taken to allow a degree of risk-taking. In the case of Mary in chapter 3, the decision was made to continue to allow her to visit local shops, but to try and increase her safety by educating her in the use of money, and in more appropriate social skills. A year later, Mary is still going to the shops regularly, still buying lots of sweets and biscuits, and has gained weight and lost two teeth as a result of decay. She has not, however, been cheated of her money, or been a victim of sexual assault.

It would be difficult to prove that the lack of sexual assault was directly related to Mary's learning about social skills. Such assaults are infrequent, and even without the additional skills Mary may not have become a victim. However, it may be that the additional education has increased the odds in her favour. The same could be said of her lack of problem with her money. She may have gained useful money-handling skills which have helped her to avoid being swindled, but she may never have been swindled anyway. Nevertheless, these are still useful skills for her to have obtained, and it may be reasonable to assume that some of the risks for Mary have been reduced.

The remaining problems centre around health issues, and these are often the most difficult to resolve. While the levels of risk involved are moderate, Mary is not doing anything more risky than many others in the population, and it is questionable whether it is ethically right to intervene in her life when one would not do so for people without learning disabilities.

Summary

Risks change constantly and people grow, change, and develop. It is important to review risk assessments regularly, and aim always to increase choice and freedom for the person with learning disabilities wherever this is possible. The only time when this should not be the first priority is when the safety of others may be put at risk. Clients who are likely to harm others need to be prevented from doing so, as well as protected from the consequences of their own lack of social controls. However, where clients are likely to put themselves at risk too there needs to be a careful assessment of where freedom ends and a duty of care begins.

Many people with learning disabilities want to have sexual relationships and some wish to become parents. These activities carry risks for them as they do for the rest of us. While everyone should be protected from exploitation, it seems unreasonable to insist on standards of understanding and decision-making from our clients that we would not apply to ourselves. If children are involved, the law rightly insists that they are protected, but here also the standards that parents with learning disabilities are required to meet may be unfairly stringent. Parents with learning disabilities need support in parenting as they do in many other areas of their lives. This does not mean than they should have to be 'super-parents' to be allowed to keep their children. Few of us are perfect parents. However, many of them could be like the rest of us – good enough – if they were given better supports.

Where people with learning disabilities have more complex problems, such as mental illness, behavioural problems, or other forms of mental disorder, they will need additional care and support to cope with their everyday lives, just as people of normal ability who have such problems do. Many of these problems impose additional risks, and these do need to be taken into account when assessing and managing risk for each person.

While proper risk-assessment procedures may be lengthy and complex, the quality of life for a person with learning disabilities is likely to depend upon them. They are there not only to protect staff, but to help people with learning disabilities to have as much choice and freedom as possible, without being put in danger unnecessarily. Thorough assessment in the initial phase should be followed by regular reviews. Just filling in a form because management require it, and putting it in a file, is never enough. If your freedom of choice depended on it, it would not be enough for you – would it?

REFERENCES

Allen, D. (2000). Recent research on physical aggression in persons with intellectual disability: An overview. *Journal of Intellectual and Developmental Disability*, 25(1), 41–57.

Beech, A. R. (1998). A psychometric typology of child abusers. *International Journal of Offender Therapy and Comparative Criminology*, 42(4), 319–39.

Bender, W. N. et al. (1999). Stress, depression and suicide among students with learning disabilities: Assessing the risk. *Learning Disability Quarterly*, 22(2), 143–56.

Cambridge, P. (1998). Challenges for safer sex education and HIV prevention in services for people with learning disabilities. *Health Promotion International*, 13(1), 67–74.

Carson, D. (1990). *Risk Taking in Mental Disorder*. London: SLE Publications.

Carson, D. (1997). Good enough risk taking. *International Review of Psychiatry*, 9, 303–8.

Feldman, M. A. and Case, L. (1999). Teaching child-care and safety skills to parents with intellectual disabilities through self-learning. *Journal of Intellectual and Developmental Disability*, 24(1), 27–45.

Gabe, J. (ed.) (1995). *Medicine, Health and Risk: Sociological Approaches*. Oxford: Blackwell.

Glaun, D. E. and Brown, P. (1999). Motherhood, intellectual disability and child protection: Characteristics of a court sample. *Journal of Intellectual and Developmental Disability*, 24(1), 95–105.

Grubin, D. (1999). Actuarial and clinical assessment of risk in sex offenders. *Journal of Interpersonal Violence*, March, 331–43.

Hawks, R. D. (1998). Practice guidelines for the assessment, management and communication of risk: A theoretical model. *American Journal of Forensic Psychology*, 16(3), 3–24.

Heilbrun, K. et al. (1999) Risk communication: Clinicians' reported approaches and perceived values. *Journal of American Academy of Psychiatry and Law*, 27(3), 397–406.

Hutton, J., Denham, J. and Clarke, C. (2000). *No Secrets*. London: HMSO.

Kemshall, H. and Pritchard, J. (eds) (1996) *Good Practice in Risk Assessment and Risk Management*. London: Jessica Kingsley.

Linke, S. (1997). *Assessing and Managing Suicide Risk*. CORE Mini-Guides. Leicester: British Psychological Society.

Lord Chancellor's Department (1997). *Who Decides: Making Decisions on Behalf of Mentally Incapacitated Adults*. CM3803. London: HMSO.

Lord Chancellor's Department (1999). *Making Decisions*. CM4465. London: HMSO.

Lupton, D. (ed.) (1999). *Risk and Sociocultural Theory: New Directions and Perspectives*. New York: Cambridge University Press.

Macpherson, G. J. (1997). Psychology and risk assessment. *British Journal of Clinical Psychology*, 36, 643–5.

McGaw, S. (1995). I Want To Be a Good Parent (series). Kidderminster: BILD Publications.

McGrath, R. J. (1991). Sex offender risk assessment and disposition planning: A review of empirical and clinical findings. *International Journal of Offender Therapy and Comparative Criminology*, 35(4), 328–50.

Monahan, J. (1997) Actuarial support for the clinical assessment of violent risk. *International Review of Psychiatry*, 9, 167–9.

Monahan, J. and Steadman, H. J. (eds) (1994). *Violence and Mental Disorder: Developments in Risk Assessment*. Chicago: Chicago University Press.

Morgan, S. (2000). *Assessing and Managing Risk*. Brighton: Pavilion Publishing.

Mulvey, E. P. (1994). Assessing evidence of a link between mental illness and violence. *Hospital and Community Psychiatry*, 45, 663–8.

Munro, E. (1999). Common errors of reasoning in child protection work. *Child Abuse and Neglect*, 23(8), 745–58.

Norman, A. (1980). *Rights and Risks*. London: Centre for Policy on Ageing.

Professional Affairs Board of the British Psychological Society (2001). *Learning Disability: Definitions and Contexts*. Leicester: British Psychological Society.

Quinsey, V. L., Harris, G. T., Rice, M. E. and Cormier, C. A. (1998). *Violent Offenders: Appraising and Managing Risk*. Washington: American Psychological Association.

Scott, J., House, R., Yates, M. and Harrington, J. (1997). Individual risk factors for early repetition of deliberate self-harm. *British Journal of Medical Psychology*, 70, 387–93.

Secretary of State for Health (2001). *Valuing People*. Government White Paper. London: HMSO.

Shergill, S. S. and Szmukler, G. (1998). How predictable is violence and suicide in community psychiatric practice? *Journal of Mental Health*, 7(4), 393–401.

Sines, D. (1987). Facing the risks in community care. *Primary Health Care*, Sept., p. 16.

Sjoeberg, L. (ed.) (1987). *Risk and Society: Studies of Risk Generation and Reactions to Risk*. London: Unwin Hyman.

Slovic, P. (1999). Trust, emotion, sex, politics and science: Surveying the risk-assessment battlefield. *Risk Analysis*, 19(4), 689–701.

Soreff, S. M. and McDuffee, M. A. (eds) (1993). *Documentation Survival Handbook for Psychiatrists and other Mental Health Professionals: A Clinician's Guide to*

Charting for Better Care, Certification, Reimbursement and Risk Management. Göttingen: Hogrefe & Huber.

Strang, D. et al. (1998). Capacity to choose place of residence: Autonomy versus beneficence? *Journal of Palliative Care*, 14(1), 25–9.

Thompson, B. L. et al. (1999). Assessment of health risk behaviours. *American Journal of Preventative Medicine*, 16(1), 48–59.

Thompson, D. J. (2000). Vulnerability, dangerousness and risk: The case of men with learning disabilities who sexually abuse. *Health, Risk and Society*, 2(1), 33–46.

Turnell, A. and Edwards, S. (1999). *Signs of Safety: A Solution and Safety Oriented Approach to Child Protection Casework.* New York: Norton.

Turner, S. (2000). Forensic risk assessment in intellectual disabilities: The evidence base and current practice in one English region. *Journal of Applied Research in Intellectual Disabilities*, 13(4), 239–55.

INDEX

Index compiled by Meg Davies